William B. Trotter

A History and Defense of African Slavery

William B. Trotter

A History and Defense of African Slavery

ISBN/EAN: 9783743385207

Manufactured in Europe, USA, Canada, Australia, Japa

Cover: Foto ©Suzi / pixelio.de

Manufactured and distributed by brebook publishing software (www.brebook.com)

William B. Trotter

A History and Defense of African Slavery

A

HISTORY AND DEFENSE

OF

AFRICAN SLAVERY.

BY

WILLIAM. B. TROTTER,
OF QUITMAN, MISSISSIPPI.

PUBLISHED FOR THE AUTHOR.
1861.

Entered, according to Act of Congress, in the year 1860, by
WILLIAM B. TROTTER,
In the Clerk's Office of the District Court of the United States for the Southern District of Mississippi.

INTRODUCTION.

As the African slave population in the United States now number about four millions, and are greatly on the increase—a population which, in the capacity of slaves, are as useful to the commerce of the world, or more so, than any other number of people of any class, and in the condition of slaves are better satisfied than in any other; and many different and erroneous opinions having been entertained, in relation to this class of people, by those who neither know anything practically or theoretically about them, in consequence of which much disturbance has been caused to exist in the political part of the different States of the United States and elsewhere for the want of the proper knowledge of the true nature and condition of African slavery, and no other book has ever been written containing as complete a history of the African race and nature of African slavery—I have written this book for the purpose of placing the subject fairly before the public in a condensed form, embracing as much information as possible in a few words.

Having been raised in a country where African slavery was tolerated, and having been the owner and manager of many of them, my opportunities for understanding their nature and disposition are equal to any other author who has ever written on the subject; and having made a careful examination into the histories and writings of able authors and eminent travelers, and procured the best information which can possibly be gleaned from the writings of others, I have embraced within this work information which will be of immense value to all classes—the non-slaveholder as well as the slaveholder—not only as to the nature and origin of African slavery, but the mode of treatment and management of African slaves, in order to make them profitable; and I am also convinced that no unprejudiced, reflecting mind can ever read this little book through, and afterward be opposed to African slavery.

WM. B. TROTTER.

CONTENTS.

CHAPTER I.

The Origin of the Negro Race.—The Descendants of Ham, the youngest Son of Noah.—The Curse pronounced on Ham and his Posterity by Noah.—Bible Evidence of Slavery...... 9

CHAPTER II.

The Utility of African Slavery, and of Slavery in the United States; and Transportation.—Further Bible Evidence of Slavery...... 25

CHAPTER III.

Nature of the African Race.—1st. His Physical Qualities; 2d. His Peculiar Color and Hair; 3d. His Mental Qualities; 4th. His Disposition and Habits...... 33

CHAPTER IV.

The Relative Condition of the African Race.—Comparison between the Wild African and American Slave...... 57

(v)

CHAPTER V.

The Probable Result as to Universal Slavery of the African Race.—All Civilized Nations would be benefited by having them as Slaves.—Their Probable Destiny.—The Destruction of the English Possessions in the West Indies by Freeing their Slaves.—Evil Result of Freeing the Slaves in San Domingo.. 67

CHAPTER VI.

The People of the Slave States, of all others, have a right to own their Slaves.—Slavery introduced by Great Britain and France into the United States.—Judicial Decisions by the Courts of Great Britain and the United States on the Subject of African Slavery................................... 76

CHAPTER VII.

The Probable Result of African Slavery......................... 117

CHAPTER VIII.

How to make African Slavery Profitable.—Treatment of Slaves.—Their Houses.—Their Clothing.—Their Food.... 120

CHAPTER IX.

How to Construct their Houses... 131

CHAPTER X.

Mode of Clothing the Slave.. 136

CHAPTER XI.

Mode of Feeding Slaves... 149

CHAPTER XII.

Women and Children—How to Treat Them....................... 155

CONTENTS. vii

CHAPTER XIII.

The Mode of arranging Out-houses on a Plantation—Jail, Ball-room, Church, Hospitals, with the Mode of Treating the Sick, and evil Consequence of the Use of Spirituous Liquors.. 164

CHAPTER XIV.

How to Treat the Women.. 181

CHAPTER XV.

A Hint to Overseers... 184

CHAPTER XVI.

Duties of Masters and Slaveholders................................. 191

CHAPTER XVII.

Free Negroes.—Their Influence and Danger among Slaves.. 199

CHAPTER XVIII.

The Conclusion, with Seven Maxims as Advice to Young Men... 202

A HISTORY AND DEFENSE

OF

AFRICAN SLAVERY.

CHAPTER I.

The Origin of the Negro Race.—The Descendants of Ham, the youngest Son of Noah.—The Curse pronounced on Ham and his Posterity by Noah.—Bible Evidence of Slavery.

When we look around us, on every side, and examine the book of nature, we find that there is a great variety of everything which meets our view or comes in contact with our senses, both in the animal and the vegetable kingdoms; and, although different things may bear in some respects a close resemblance to each other, in other respects they are very widely different, and intended for very different uses. Thus, we find in the vegetable kingdom many kinds of oaks, many kinds of willows, many kinds of hickories, many kinds of corn, and of everything we behold many kinds of the same species. So among animals, from the smallest insect up to man, many kinds of each, in some respects alike, in others very widely different. Thus, we find that the greyhound, though very swift, cannot scent like the long-eared hound; neither can the bull-dog scent like the one or run as the other, but he is better adapted to fight than either. God has made them as they are, and each have their particular duties to perform, and it would be perfectly absurd for either to attempt to cope with the other in the particular occupation for which God has formed them; hence, when we look at a tree, we find that it has bark, sap, heart, root, trunk and branches, all different from each other, yet the whole combined forms the tree, neither able to perform the duties of the others, yet all in the performance of the duties assigned to each add to the life and nutriment of the whole. So with the human system; there is the head, the hands, the body, the legs and the feet, besides many other portions, each having a separate duty; none able to perform the duties of the rest, none able to do without the others, yet all combined makes the man complete. It would not do for all to be head, neither for all to be hands, legs or feet, but it is all-important that there should be a due proportion of each, and no one portion can say to any of the rest, I have no need of thee.

So it is in society; there must be some to govern and some to be governed; there must be some to trade, some to navigate the seas, some to cultivate the soil, and some to manufacture, and all combined adds to the benefit of themselves and each other; and thus has God formed all things according to his good pleasure and for his own glory. Some men he has made black, some red, and some white; some he has made wise, and some he has made for one purpose and some for another; and we can no more raise the negro to the equality of the white man than we could change the color of his skin, or the form of his hair, or the circulation of his blood.

The next question will then arise as to the origin of the different races of men, as it respects the three colors—the black, the red, and the white man. These seem to be the three distinct races of men, differing materially in color, in disposition, in intellect, and in habit. We read in the Book of Genesis that God formed Adam, the first man, out of the dust of the earth, and breathed into his nostrils the breath of life, and that God brought on him a deep sleep and took a rib from his side, out of which he formed a woman and gave her to the man; that they were both placed in the Garden of Eden, and commanded that of a particular tree of the garden they should not eat of the fruit thereof; that by the temptation of the devil they were induced to partake of the forbidden fruit, and thereby fell from their state of purity and were driven out of the garden in consequence of their disobedience; that they soon began to multiply, until there were a great many human beings on the earth; that the human race became very wicked, and God was offended at them; that in consequence of which, God destroyed, by means of the flood, all the human race from the face of the earth except Noah and his family, who were saved by means of an ark which God had instructed Noah to build; that Noah had three sons, to wit, Shem, Ham, and Japheth, with their families, from whom sprang all the human race which has since inhabited the earth; and there can be little doubt but that God created the different colors of men in that noted family; that as he intended to repeople the earth after the flood by the family of Noah, and wrought a miracle in their preservation, he also wrought a miracle in the formation of the different colors in the three sons of Noah; hence, it is generally agreed by all authors on the subject, from the best authority we can obtain, that Shem was a red man, and that he is the same with Melchizedek—mentioned as a great high priest in the Bible, for he preached to the descendants of Noah for four hundred years after the flood, and was held in great reverence; that Ham was a black man, and took his name from his color, for the word Ham means black; and that Japheth was a white man. Thus, in this remarkable family, the family of Noah, from the best authority we have, commenced the different races of men.

After the waters of the flood had subsided, Noah planted a vineyard, (see Genesis, 9th chapter, from the 20th to the 27th verse inclusive;) and being on one occasion drunk by drinking too freely of the wine, Ham, one of his sons, seeing him lie thus exposed naked, made sport of him and pointed him out to Shem and Japheth, his two brothers, who took a garment and walked backwards and covered their father; in consequence of which, Noah, when he came to himself, pronounced this curse on Ham, to wit, 25th verse: Cursed be Canaan; a servant of servants shall he be unto his brethren.

26th v. And he said, Blessed be the Lord God of Shem; and Canaan shall be his servant.

27th v. God shall enlarge Japheth, and he shall dwell in the tents of Shem; and Canaan shall be his servant.

Ham, the black son of Noah, who was called Canaan, settled Africa, and the curse pronounced on him by his father, on that memorable occasion, is verified by the enslavery of his posterity down to the present day.

The first introduction of Africans into the United States was not a matter of haste, but the subject was deliberately investigated and

NOAH AND HIS SONS.

entered upon by wise men and philanthropists. Shortly after the settling of the colonies by Great Britain, in North America, a skillful navigator, by the name of Hudson, suggested to some of the nobility of England and France that the African race was peculiarly adapted to hard, rough work, such as clearing land and making fences, and if properly trained they might be made of great value in the performance of the rough work in the colonies, and the trade would be a profitable one and pay well for the capital invested; that it would redound to the good of the African as well as the white man; that the African kings were in the habit of killing promiscuously all of their prisoners, and sometimes would eat them for food, and that if they could procure the value of a hog of the same weight, they would gladly make the exchange, and thereby the life of man, a poor unfortunate prisoner, would be saved and be taken to a Christian land, where he would hear the gospel preached and have an opportunity of becoming a Christian. This seemed very feasible to the nobility, but they were unwilling to embark in the speculation unless they could become thoroughly convinced that it was morally right for them to engage in such a speculation.

Consequently, as some of them were of the Roman Catholic religion, they sent a special delegation to the Pope of Rome, and asked his opinion on the subject, whether or not it was right for them to transport Africans to the colonies in order to make slaves of them. The Pope, after mature deliberation, replied that he had searched the Scriptures and maturely considered the subject, and that he found, on examining the ninth chapter of the Book of Genesis, that Noah had pronounced a curse upon Ham, that he positively should be a servant of servants, and that the African race were the descendants of Ham, and that it was right and proper in a moral point of view for them to engage in the business, and, as far as he was concerned, he would grant them the privilege; in consequence of which a company was then formed by the nobility of England and some of the French nobility with the navigator Hudson to embark in the slave trade. A few vessels were fitted out in New York and Boston and sent to the coast of Africa for slaves; the vessels were gone but a short time before they returned, well stored with slaves which cost them but a trifle, and they were soon disposed of at a very large profit in New York and Boston. Hence originated the first traffic in African slaves in the United States; but they had been dealt with as slaves in Africa and many other places long before.

When they were first brought on board the vessel, they supposed that the white people intended to eat them, and had bought them for food; as many of the African tribes eat their prisoners, they supposed that the white people would do so likewise. But great was their surprise and joy when they were informed that they were intended to work, and would be treated with humanity and kindness as friends. Most of them were entirely naked when purchased, and others had only a small piece of raw hide on their hips to hide their nakedness; and when they were clothed and informed that they were intended as slaves, that if they behaved well they would be protected by their masters, clothed, fed, and properly cared for, they could scarcely be made to believe it; and after they were convinced of the fact, not one could be induced to return to their old condition, but rejoiced that they had been rescued from the hands of their own race, and saved from the horrid fate of being eaten by the Africans.

African slavery is objected to by some, because they say it is morally wrong for one individual to keep another as a slave to serve him. To such I would say, where do you go to get your moral code, is it not to the Bible? It certainly is to the Bible, the great book of morals and religion, we must all look for the best code of morals which has ever been given to the human race. Then if you believe the Bible, you must believe that African slavery is right, and that slavery existed in the world long before America was discovered by Columbus, and was very common among the Jews immediately after their entrance into the promised land. That it is entirely consistent with the doctrine of the Holy Bible, see Leviticus, chap. 25th, verses 44, 45, and 46, which reads thus: Both thy bondmen and thy bondmaids, which thou shalt have, shall be of the heathen that are round about you; of them shall ye buy bondmen and bondmaids. Moreover, of the children of the strangers that do sojourn among you, of them shall ye buy and of their families that are with you, which they begat in your land; and they shall be your possession. And ye shall take them as an inheritance for your children after you, to inherit them for a possession; they shall be your bondmen forever.

Thus we find that the children of Israel were not only permitted to make slaves or bondmen of the heathen, but actually commanded so to do, and that such should be their bondmen to them and their children forever.

And, as before observed, the Africans are heathens, the descendants of Ham; that the different races of men commenced with the family of Noah; that Shem was red, Ham black, and Japheth a white man; and that a miracle was wrought in the birth of Noah's three sons, as well as in the preservation of that family from the destruction of the flood; that as the earth was to be repeopled by the family of Noah, God formed the different races in that peculiar family according to his good will and pleasure, and suited the different branches for the purposes for which they were designed. That we are warranted in coming to this conclusion, is very evident. The word Ham means black; thus, Ham being black at his birth, and of different color from any other individual, was called after his color; and not only this, his descendants are also, in most cases, distinguished by kinky wool on their heads, like a merino sheep, only it is black and coarse; other races have hair on their heads. Thus it seems that Ham, the black son of Noah, possessed a color in conformity with his disposition, for he was certainly very vile and base to have treated his father with such indignity as he did in making sport of him, and pointing him out as an object of ridicule. Ham was noticed by his two brothers to rush out of his father's tent almost bursting with laughter; but as soon as the fit had somewhat abated, Shem and Japheth made inquiry respecting the cause of so much mirth and uproar, when they found that their father, Noah, was laying naked, exposed; finding a garment, they seized it and placed it on their shoulders and walked backward and covered him with it; when Noah awoke from his wine and knew what his youngest son had done unto him, he said: Cursed be Canaan, (Ham;) a servant of servants shall he be unto his brethren. And he said, Blessed be the Lord God of Shem; and Canaan (Ham) shall be his servant. God shall enlarge Japheth, and he shall dwell in the tents of Shem; and Canaan (Ham) shall be his servant.

But, lest the reader should become perplexed respecting the application of this anathema, on account of the text above referred to being in the English, cursed Canaan, instead of cursed Ham, as it should have been translated, we state that the Arabic copy of the Book of Genesis, which is a language of equal authority with the Hebrew, and originally the very same, reads, Cursed be Ham, the father of Canaan; a servant of servants shall he be unto his brethren.

In this sense it has ever been understood by all the commentators, in every age, on the sacred writings. Bishop Newton thus understood the passage, who also refers the reader to the Arabic Bible for the true reading, as does also Adam Clark.

This light and frivolous disposition of Ham, and great want of filial respect for his parents, has extended itself to his whole posterity. The negroes of the United States and Africa, and elsewhere, are all given to loud laughter, game-making, and sport with everything around them, and a great want of reverence or respect for parents; they will frequently laugh at trivial matters so loud that they can be heard at the distance of half a mile or more. After the flood, Shem, who became a high priest, and is by historians considered to be the same as Melchizedek, preached to the increasing population of the descendants of Noah; but Ham and his posterity gave no heed to him, but forsook the true religion and became idolators, and thus became the most base, vile, and degraded of all others of the human race. Bowen, in his travels in Central Africa, says that he found some cities containing sixty thousand inhabitants, and some of them had their farms as far distant as twenty miles, and none of them even possessed so much as a sled to haul it in with, but packed their provisions on their backs, entirely destitute of any of the improvements in arts and sciences; they live in little mud huts, made of mud and sticks, and many of them go naked winter and summer, as the beast of the forest, and feed on lizards, snakes, or any vile thing they can get hold of, and are entirely void of chastity, giving a loose rein to their animal passions; they cohabit promiscuously with one another, and their lust is not confined to one another, but in many cases, men with each other, and with beasts; they are continually at war, one tribe with another, and they do not scruple to eat each other as quick as they would eat a bit of a hog or a monkey; in their market-places they frequently have the limbs of each other hung up in the stall for sale as they would a sheep or a pig; and thus in this degraded, fallen state they live, devoid of religion, morals, or even common decency; and therefore the great necessity of the balance of mankind who feel for the sufferings of human beings, and would wish to ameliorate their woes and bring to a knowledge of the truth and of the religion of Jesus Christ, uniting in their efforts to bring them in a state of slavery to Christian masters, who will correct their morals, feed and clothe them, and make them work and cultivate the soil, so as to become useful to themselves and the balance of mankind. This can only be done by first reducing them to a state of slavery; missionaries have heretofore been sent among them to no purpose; they pay no attention to their teachings, but frequently kill and eat them for food.

CHAPTER II.

The Utility of African Slavery, and of Slavery in the United States; and Transportation.—Further Bible Evidence of Slavery.

That the African is only an incumberer of the ground in his wild and native state, needs only to be pointed to, in the wilds of Africa; for although it contains a population of perhaps two hundred millions of souls, they produce nothing for transportation; they manufacture nothing; they invent nothing; the wild African is but a little ahead of the orang-outang in his habits. They possess a fine fertile country, yet it is comparatively uncultivated. The African possesses a strong frame, a robust constitution, a fertile country, and delightful climate; yet he walks about, up and down in the forest, as naked as when he came into the world, feeding on fruits and reptiles, fills himself and lays down and sleeps, and then rises and pursues the same course again, occasionally meeting with the child of an enemy and killing and eating it as he would a rabbit or squirrel; and such is his native condition. But when they are taken by the white people and taught to work in the field, they are clothed and fed as human beings, they become as a matter of necessity civilized, and, by frequently hearing the gospel preached, they become Christianized and elevated far above their former condition in the scale of human beings. By their labor they become very useful, and add greatly to the commerce of the world. In the United States there are now, in A.D. 1860, about three and a half millions of African slaves, the proceeds of whose labor contribute, in exports to foreign countries, more than one-half of the exports in value of all the exports of the nation. In the single article of cotton alone, the nation exports 3,500,000 bales, which, at $50 per bale, is worth $175,000,000, the proceeds of slave labor, besides tobacco, sugar, and flour, and many other articles, which would amount to more than fifty millions more—making a sum-total of exports from slave labor alone amount to over two hundred and twenty millions of dollars annually, from the United

States to other countries, besides what is consumed at home, bringing in return the products and manufactures of other countries an amount equivalent in exchange for their exports; thus giving an impetus to trade and commerce of the world and manufactories of more than four hundred millions of dollars annually, by being kept in a state of servitude and made to cultivate the soil, for which they were intended; while the whole population of Africa, with her two hundred millions of people in a free and savage state, exports nothing, adds nothing, does nothing for themselves or others. I speak of Africa proper, the kinky heads, which comprise a large portion. If there is any place in Africa which bids fair to achieve anything in the way of civilization and the arts, it is the little colony of Liberia, peopled by about six thousand American slaves who have been sent over from the United States: and they feel as much above the common wild African as a white man would above his slave, or more so; and should they be left to themselves, without the fostering care of the white man, would soon degenerate into their ancient barbarism with the rest of the natives. Thus we see, that for the good of the African himself, for the welfare of mankind in general, that the African may be well provided for while he lives, and brought to a condition where he may become a Christian, and the welfare of his immortal soul promoted by hearing the gospel preached, and that he may become useful and happy in his sphere of existence, it is absolutely necessary that he should be made a slave of and placed under a master, who will correct him for his faults and teach him to behave himself as a human being, and make him work for his support. A negro will never construct a steam-engine or a railroad, or make any new addition to anything of the kind; yet with a good overseer he can dig up the iron ore, aid in melting it; can dig in the ground and aid in making a railroad, and add as much in the construction of it as white men, with some one to construct and direct; and in a state of slavery do as much towards internal improvements and promoting the arts and sciences as white men, while in a free state they would not strike a lick or do anything. Therefore, the three and a half millions of slaves in the United States are doing more for the commerce of the nation, its internal improvement at home, and the promotion of industry in the manufacturing nations of the earth, than the same number of people of any color on any part of the globe. Then, is it not right, is it not proper, is it not perfectly in conformity with religion and the doctrine of the Holy Bible, that the African should be placed in bondage to the white man—the only condition in which it seems he can exist as a moral human being and be provided for, or in any manner content, useful, or happy? It seems to me, that no reflecting, rational man can doubt for a moment the absolute necessity of making him a slave—for which he was intended. But, it is contended, that even if this should be the case, that the African is more useful, more happy, and better provided for in a state of slavery than when free, that unless we can find that it is in accordance with the doctrine of the Bible, it is morally wrong. To this, I would again refer the reader to Leviticus, xxv. 44-46 verses: Both thy bondmen and thy bondmaids, which thou shalt have, shall be of (from, in Hebrew) the heathen that are around about you; of (from) them shall ye buy bondmen and bondmaids. Moreover, of (from) the children of the strangers that do sojourn among you, of them shall you buy, and of their families that are with you, which they begat in your land; and they shall be your possession, and ye shall take them as an inheritance for your children after you to inherit them for a possession; they shall be your bondmen forever: but over your brethren the children of Israel ye shall not rule, one over another with rigor. This shows that the servitude is perpetual. They shall be your bondmen forever. *Le olaum*, and the heathen bondmen are transmitted as property by inheritance to the children.

There is in the Hebrew language, as well as Hebrew society, two classes of servants, represented by two distinct words indicative of different positions or relations. These are hired servants and bondmen; the former is represented by one word and the latter by another; these are of different meaning and origin.

A hired servant, in the law of Moses, is called *sacheer;* a bondman or bond-servant is uniformly denominated *gehved:* the latter is never called *sacheer,* nor the former *gehved.* Like *doulos* in the Septuagint and in the New Testament, *gehved* includes divers sorts of servants not receiving wages, but *sacheer* indicates simply a hired servant.

They are sometimes found in the same verse in contrast, Leviticus, xxv. 39 : If thy brother that dwelleth by thee become poor, and be sold to thee, thou shalt not compel him to serve as a *gehved,* a bond-servant, but as a *sacheer,* a hired servant. Again, verse 42: He shall not be sold as a *gehved,* a bondman. Verse 44: Of the heathen thou shalt or mayest buy bondmen, *gehved.* Thus, it is clear, that among the Jews there were two kinds of servants: *gehved,* the bond-servant, or slave as we term it, and *sacheer,* the hired servant; and both classes were tolerated by the laws of Moses, and nowhere condemned in the New Testament. Taking then the Bible as it is, we nowhere find anything condemning the principle of slavery of the heathen; but we find it has been tolerated and permitted by the laws of Moses, as laid down in the Holy Bible, and practiced by the Jews, the favored people of God; and by others so long that the memory of man runneth not to the contrary; and our observation teaches us, from fair illustration, that the African race is elevated in the scale of human beings by being placed in a state of bondage; that they are only useful when thus situated; that they are more happy, better provided for, more moral, better satisfied in that state, and prefer it to any other.

CHAPTER III.

Nature of the African race—1st. His Physical Qualities; 2d. His Peculiar Color and Hair; 3d. His Mental Qualities; 4th. His Disposition and Habits.

IN many respects the African negro or kinky heads differ materially from the white people, and the Indian or red man, in his physical as well as his mental capacity. The negro is generally stouter built, possessing heavier muscles and harder bones than either the white man or the Indian; the bones of the negro are more firm and much harder to break, and the skull of the negro is thicker, as has been frequently proven by anatomists by investigation: and a blow on the head, which would kill a white man or an Indian, will scarcely stagger a negro, which shows conclusively that he is particularly intended to perform the rough, heavy work of the world, and to endure hardships. The head of the negro is also different in shape from any other: they are generally flat on top and low in front; and the skull can easily be distinguished from any other, both from the peculiar shape and thickness. They generally have more robust frames and stouter chests than any other race. The pure negro is jet black, or nearly so, has black, kinky wool, somewhat coarser than that of a coarse wool sheep, black eyes, and a flat nose without any gristle on the point. I can tell a negro in the dark, merely by feeling his nose; he has also a flat foot, without much hollow, and a long heel; a negro's track is easily distinguished from any other. These are prominent traits in his formation, which are easily discerned; but there are many other material differences in his physical formation from that of any other class of the human race. He is not as susceptible to disease as the other races, and is capable of bearing more fatigue and for a greater length of time, and requires less sleep than either of the other races; when they sleep their sleep is very sound, and they are very hard to wake, but they are soon refreshed by it. They will often work all day, from daylight until dark, only stopping long enough to eat their meals, doing the heaviest kind of labor, and after their masters have retired to rest at night, after ten o'clock, will put out from home and stroll about in the neighborhood six or seven miles round, and return home about three hours before day, sit down by the fire and nod until daybreak, jump up and be ready to go to work again, work all day and run about again at night, the next as before, without experiencing the least inconvenience.

Such hardship as would completely prostrate a white man does not appear to affect them in the least. Among the slaves of the United States there are a great many different shades of color—from the deep black or full-blooded Africans to the bright mulatto; but all other shades brighter than the deep black is caused by amalgamation, or mixing of the white blood with the black, and not at all from the climate. The full-blooded African will retain his black color anywhere for any length of time without any change, and also the kinky heads without any respect to climate; and it is immaterial where they are born, the children will be as black as their ancestors, and possess every other quality of their ancestors; and when crossed with the white race, they partake more of the negro than the white man, both in complexion and disposition. In stature, the kinky-headed negro is about the height of English or American, varying from five feet in height to six feet six inches; and although they are generally much stouter and heavier muscled, yet, in general, they are not as active as the white race, and cannot run so fast, but can hold out much longer. I knew a negro boy, about twelve years old, who was stationed at a plantation in Clark County, Mississippi, and his mother was at another place sixteen miles distant; and he would often run away and run his best the whole sixteen miles, going at the rate of about eight miles an hour, and at the end of the sixteen miles did not seem to be the least tired or fatigued. The average weight of the African man is from one hundred and forty to two hundred pounds. They are much stouter and stronger, physically, than the Dutch, the French, the Germans, Spaniards, or any other race; the English and Americans are the nearest to them in point of physical strength than any other, while at the same time they have less intellect than either of these races, which shows very clearly that they were not intended to construct, but to labor under the instruction of others.

The mental faculties of the African are not so great as either of the other races of men, although in a physical point of view they are unsurpassed; they seem to be incapable of much reflection, and almost void of any inventive genius whatever. Although Africa has been settled as long as any other quarter of the globe, with a fertile soil and abounding in minerals of many descriptions, and a soil which is capable of most improvement by cultivation, there never has as yet emanated from a full-blooded, kinky-headed African any useful invention, or any improvement in the arts and sciences, by which themselves or the balance of mankind were the least benefited or improved, either in mechanics, commerce, the invention of implements of labor, the improvement thereon, advancement in agriculture, the improvement in morals or otherwise; and I defy contradiction to the contrary. Although they have frequently witnessed the improvements going on in the surrounding nations, and had specimens of the productions of other countries distributed among them, and the benefit of literary travelers frequently among them, they have made no advances in civilization or the arts and sciences. Of those in the United States in a state of slavery, some of them have been taught to become tolerably good, rough mechanics, so that they could do good, rough plantation work, stock a plow in a rough manner, shoe a horse, frame a house, make a brick chimney, etc.; but in every case the work is rough and will not bear close inspection. There never has been a full-blooded negro who has ever yet been able to compete with a skillful white man in any of the fine arts; and I think it impossible that there ever will be: any more than that the moon can ever shine as bright as the sun. The African may be greatly improved from his native state of education by cultivating his mind and giving him suitable instructions, as is evidenced by the great superiority of the American slave over the wild African in his native state in Africa, both in morals, intelligence, and religion; but they can no more be made equal with the white man than a piece of coarse sandstone can be made equal to the beautiful marble, or a piece of rough iron brought to the pure state of the gold; or that his skin can be changed from black to white, or his kinky wool to beautiful, straight hair, by education. Man may polish, but God makes the material.

Then, as to the disposition of the African race, they are savages, and their disposition has a downward tendency; naturally inclined to degenerate, as the stone that is tossed in the air has a tendency to fall to the earth—as long as it is held up by force, it will stay up, but as soon as let go, it will naturally fall to the earth; so, as long as the African is forced into a state of civilization by the white man and kept up, he will be more or less civilized; but as soon as left to himself, he will naturally return gradually to his ancient state of barbarism. If all of the American slaves were turned loose in Africa, with all the advantages they now possess, with the knowledge they have of the arts and sciences, and the knowledge of the Christian religion, they would soon eclipse all

Africa in their improvements, and subjugate the whole country by their knowledge; but they would immediately commence degenerating, and in the course of two or three generations would degenerate into dark, heathenish barbarism, and be as barbarous, ignorant, base, and vile as the present population of Africa. They are actuated, in most instances, in their actions, by the disposition of fear, and have no disposition or inclination to respect or obey those who permit them to act as they please; they prefer a tyrant for a master to any other; provided he will treat them with kindness, it matters not how hard they are compelled to work, or what hardships they are made to endure, if their owners will feed them well and clothe them, and protect them; the more rigid he is with them, and the better discipline he establishes among them, the better they will love him, and the more useful they will be to him. They are naturally inclined to be filthy in their habits, and negligent, careless, and wasteful, and it requires the strictest kind of attention on the part of their owners to keep them in order, and to make them take care of their clothing and keep themselves cleanly, and to be made even to attend to their own children; of the two in the United States, the master is often the greatest slave in attending to the welfare of his slaves, nursing them when sick and administering to their comforts; this is all-important on the part of the owner, for the negro will pay but little attention to their nearest relatives when sick, unless compelled to do so. They are naturally inclined to be base and profligate in their habits, and consider a free and promiscuous exercise of their sexual passions as the height of all human happiness and glory; and it requires the most rigid discipline on the part of their owners to prevent marriages between brother and sister, and illicit intercourse between parent and child, and even between one male and another; and notwithstanding the most rigid discipline, they will frequently commit rapes on each other's children; frequently on females under ten years old; they seem to inherit this unrestrained sexual appetite from their ancestors, and look no higher for happiness; but owing to the restrictions placed on them by their owners, the constant admonitions to lead a moral and upright life, and the good examples continually set before the American, they are much less lewd and far better in their practice in this behalf than the free African in the wilds of Africa, who indulge in an unrestrained manner in every species of debauchery of that kind; and then feed upon the flesh of each other, as upon that of a squirrel or monkey. It is an evident fact, that by the fostering care of the owners of slaves, they increase in the United States upwards of ten per cent. faster than the whites, according to population. as shown by the census of 1840 and 1836, while from every account we receive, the African race has been on the decrease in Africa for many years past, owing to their sinful, base, and corrupt habits. The African has but little of the principles of sympathy about him, and when clothed with authority becomes the most overbearing tyrant in the world, and will frequently abuse their authority by inflicting punishment in a cruel manner, merely to show their authority. I have known owners of slaves to select the most wise and discreet among them as overseers, or drivers as they are termed, to look over and watch the balance, with power to whip when they misbehave; and as certain as a white man would visit the field, just so certain the black driver would begin to whip and lash the slaves, whether they deserved it or not, just to show his authority, until the owner would stop him, if present, or he would be rebuked by the white man for his unfeeling cruelty. Hence the saying, when a man gets into office and commences showing his authority by cruel and arbitrary actions, that he is like a negro driver in a corn-field; this expression conveys all that is necessary in describing the most bigoted tyrant.

The African has an inclination to be a slave, and really prefers that condition to any other; they cannot bear responsibility, and when they are well fed and clothed, and kept in order, they are decidedly the happiest and best contented people in the world; and will fight for their masters in a hurry. It is altogether a mistake, that if the negroes should become the most numerous in a great proportion, that they would rebel and murder their masters and seek to be free; this is not the case. If the negroes were in proportion of a thousand to one white man, the white man would still keep them in slavery with as much ease as he now does, because the negroes prefer bondage to freedom, as has been evinced on various occasions. In many instances, it is true, that occasionally there will be restless spirits among them, who will occasionally rise up and do mischief, and sometimes murder their masters; but they are of very rare occurrence; and in a majority of cases, young white men are raised up on the plantation with their slaves, and they become attached to each other, and there is a feeling of relationship existing between them, which makes them feel very near and dear to each other, and the slave would risk his life for his master's welfare sooner than for the nearest relation he had, and looks to his master as his only friend and protector; while, on the other hand, although the master would correct his slave for his faults when necessary, would risk his life in the defense of his slave sooner than let him be unjustly abused. As an evidence of the preference of the African race for a state of slavery to any other, they are held in bondage by each other in Africa as well as elsewhere, and make the worst and most cruel of masters to each other; the Indians also in the Chocktaw nation own many of them; also the Creek, and Cherokee Indians, west of the Mississippi River; some of these red men of the forest own over two hundred African slaves, owned by single individuals; the Spaniards also, in Cuba, own a great many; yet they quietly submit to slavery—even prefer it to any other state, even to serve the wild, red man of the forest.

A man by the name of Stroud, about the year 1836, carried five hundred slaves from the State of South Carolina into the northern part of Texas, before the State of Texas was annexed to the United States, at a time when the Cherokee Indians were in a state of hostilities to the whites, and settled right on the borders of the hostile Cherokee country; he armed all of his negroes with a good gun, taught them the use of fire-arms; had two cannon, taught them their use, mustered them every day, and whipped the Cherokees in several engagements with his negroes; in a wild country, where there was no other white man within one hundred miles of him, and the negroes only had to kill him off to be as free as the Indians; yet they stuck to him, and looked to him as their only chance of safety and protection, and served him as faithful as if he had been surrounded by an army of a thousand men for his protection, and would have killed any man who would have dared to injure their master. Does not this show a preference for that condition on the part of the blacks? It certainly does, in the strongest colors; and clearly shows that the Africans are destined to be slaves, and are satisfied and useful in that condition and no other.

Again, a gentleman by the name of Prince, who lives near Bladen Springs, in the State of Alabama, a few years before this, went to England on some business for the State, and carried with him a servant, a negro man named Tom; when he got to England he told Tom that he was as free as his master, and he would advise him to remain; that if he would remain in England, he would give him five hundred dollars to make a start in the world, and he might eventually become a wealthy man; Tom told his master that he did not wish to remain on any terms, but was determined to return with him, and remain his slave; his master told him to look around, that he would be in England for several weeks, and if Tom should determine to stay, that he could do so. During the six weeks which he remained in England, Tom had considerable attention paid to him, and many inducements held out to him to remain by some of the abolitionists, and his master would frequently importune him to remain. One day Tom had taken an excursion into the country to see how the common poor folks lived, as he called them; and after visiting an Irish settlement, he became alarmed, and was afraid that his master intended to leave him in England against his will; and went to him with tears in his eyes, and told him not to think of leaving him in England, or anywhere else; that he could not bear the idea of being separated from him; that five hundred dollars would be no inducement with his freedom for him to remain; that the poor folks in England were worse off ten times than the black folks in the United States; that the slaves in the United States were cared for and provisioned by their masters, while the poor folks in England were worse slaves in reality than the slaves in the United States, and had to supply themselves with food and clothing, or starve and go naked.

While in England, Tom would frequently speak of his master's possessions in the United States, and spoke of them as his own, and assumed a considerable degree of consequence, more than his master did, as negroes always do; they pride themselves on their masters' possessions, and assume a consequence according to what they consider the consequence of their owner; and frequently take the title of their masters, as Colonel, Judge, or General, and appear much prouder of their title than their masters, who really have the office and title. It is amusing, at times, to see them at church, or out on some public occasion; their masters often indulge them a great deal, where they are faithful, and they generally are provided with a fine suit of clothes to wear on Sundays and on public occasions. To see them dressed out in a suit of fine broadcloth, with a white linen shirt and fine cambric ruffles, with a pair of white kid gloves on, and an umbrella in their hands to keep off the sun, strutting about as large as life, with a pair of red-topped boots on, while their masters present a plain, country gentleman, dressed in plain homespun of his own make. The negro likes to have a rich master, and cannot bear to be called poor folks' negro; and they would run away from a man who only owns one slave, no matter how well he is treated, or on what equality, to get on a plantation where there are many, regardless of how hard the fare may be; a negro would prefer a master who owned a hundred slaves, if he get nothing but bread to eat, where he would be confined to hard labor from daylight to dark, to one who only owned him, one who would give him all the dainties of the world to eat, have them cooked for him, and would clothe him well, and give him half of his time to work for himself; they would run away from such an owner to get to the rich man. They have the most dire contempt for the poor, ignorant classes of white people, and call them poor bucra; but with an intelligent gentleman, who only owns one as a body-servant, they are generally satisfied to remain, yet never grieve at being sold to a wealthier master who owns a great number of slaves.

I knew an instance of a man by the name of Brock, who owned a negro man and two other negroes, one a woman and the other a boy. Brock and his negro man Charles were raised up together, and wrestled and sported together in their boyhood; the consequence was, Brock permitted his negro man Charles to do very much as he pleased; Charles only worked when his master did, eat what his master eat, and was just about as free to act. Charles naturally looked with contempt on his master, as being no better than himself, and wished his master to sell him to some rich man who owned more slaves; his master refused to do so, and the consequence was, Charles ran away, was gone several weeks, and at length was caught by one of the neighbors, who tied him, and in taking him home, had to cross a large creek in a ferry flat; in crossing the creek, Charles jumped into the stream and tried to commit suicide by drowning himself, but was pulled out before he had time to drown. alleging that he had rather die than to belong to so poor a man as his master. His master finding that Charles was determined in his resolution, sold him to a man in the neighborhood, who owned about thirty slaves, and who seldom gave them anything more than bread to eat, worked them very hard, and allowed them but few privileges, where Charles, in his new situation, seemed perfectly satisfied and contented, having procured a master for whom he had respect.

Another instance of the kind occurred with a negro man I had in my charge, by the name of George, who belonged to my brother's estate, and the law required him to be hired out. George was one of the best and most truthful and faithful black men I ever knew, and I hired him to a man in the neighborhood of Quitman, in the State of Mississippi, by the name of Murphy, who had no other slaves on his premises, and was a very humane man, and treated George in every way as one equal; he gave him plenty to eat, and only required him to work when he worked, and was very kind to him. George stood it about two weeks, when one day he went to Mr. M. and told him he wanted him to hire him out to some white man who owned negroes; that he was too lonesome, and really could not stand it any longer. Mr. M. asked him if he was dissatisfied with his fare: he answered he was not, but, on the contrary, Mr. M. had treated him as well and as kind as he could wish, and he could ask no more; but he wanted to be where there were more negroes; that he would prefer being on a large farm with a multitude of negroes, and eating nothing but bread, than to be situated where he was, with all the dainties of the world. The consequence was, that George would not be satisfied until Murphy had to rehire him, and put him on a farm where there were many other slaves; where George seemed perfectly satisfied with short ration, and cooked it himself.

I will also mention another instance of somewhat similar nature. Gen. Alexander Trotter owned a slave at the time of his death, by the name of Willoughby, a very trustworthy man, very intelligent and sprightly; and being the owner of a great many slaves, he made Willoughby his overseer, who, under the superintendence of his master, soon acquired the reputation of being a great overseer and an excellent manager. Having rich land to cultivate, a great many hands, and making large crops, Willoughby was very attentive to his business, and became a great favorite with his master, so much so, that when his master died, in A.D. 1847, he made his will and gave Willoughby his freedom, and willed him, in addition, about one thousand dollars' worth of property, and a forty-acre tract of land as a residence. As soon as Willoughby became free and in possession of a decent competency, he became very much dissatisfied and reckless, commenced drinking, and soon became a great drunkard and quite a nuisance, having spent a great portion of what his master had given him, in the course of two or three years. He said he felt very unhappy, and did not know what to do; that he was once a happy man, in the lifetime of his master, when he had some person to look up to and protect him; but now it seemed to him that no one cared for him, and was sorry his master was gone; that if every negro felt as he did, that none of them would ever wish to be free; that he had been miserable ever since he had his freedom. I told him that I was sorry to see him throwing himself away, and acting so badly, as I once used to own him, and had sold him to my brother; that I would take him under my charge, and give him land on my farm to cultivate and manage for him, and he would have to walk straight, and conduct properly, or I would flog him. I then took him under my charge, and fixed him up comfortably, and gave him as much land as he could cultivate; made him go to work, and forbid him the use of spirituous liquors, and kept him in restraint; when he became steady and industrious in his habits, and is growing rich, and is quite a decent man.

This shows how little they are qualified to act for themselves, and the great necessity of having some one to control them and keep them in order; that when properly managed and kept under the proper restraint, they are as useful as any other class of the community, and the most happy by far; but when set free, they are not qualified to manage for themselves, and soon become nuisances to society, and a burden and a pest to the community, and the most degraded and unhappy people in the universe.

Suppose, then, that there are now two hundred and twenty millions of Africans in the wilds of Africa, who are like drones in the bee-hive, adding nothing to the commerce of the world; roaming wild in the forest, many as naked as when they entered into existence, feeding upon reptiles and upon the flesh of each other, ignorant of the religion of Jesus Christ, and practicing all of the abominations which their ingenuity can invent or their appetites crave; that twenty millions of these black people were taken and made slaves of; that they were put under good masters, who would take care of them, feed and clothe them, and make them work, and teach them the Christian religion, and raise them from their present state of savage degradation and wickedness to the level of the American slave; that they could be rendered as useful to themselves and the balance of the world in the same proportion in numbers as the American slaves now are; the consequence would be, that they would add twelve hundred millions of dollars more to the worth and commerce of the world annually than it now has, and would give an impetus to trade, commerce, and manufacturing in every civilized nation of the earth unheard of, or unthought of before; and they would be far better provided for and attended to than they can ever possibly be in the wilds of Africa in their present condition.

CHAPTER IV.

The Relative Condition of the African Race.—Comparison between the Wild African and American Slave.

When we take a view of Africa and its population, the situation of the country, with its advantages, and behold the degradation, the barbarism, ignorance, vice, profligacy, indolence, superstition, bigotry, and wretchedness of its population, we are at once surprised and amazed at the very wide difference which exist between the blacks in that country and the black slave in America; to see how very far ahead of them the American slave is advanced in civilization, morality, and religion; and we are again as much surprised that any human being in a civilized country, professing to be the follower of the Lord Jesus Christ, and an advocate of his holy religion, and a lover of peace and morality, should ever be an abolitionist, or desire to free the slaves of America and reduce them to such state of degradation and vice, from the high position they now occupy, compared to the wild African, and from their present happy and useful condition; that they should turn unheedingly from Africa, where human degradation, vice, and misery exists in all forms; where they might do much good by their efforts in ameliorating the suffering of the poor wild African, and with a false pretended sympathy pity the condition of the American slaves, and with a false notion of religion seek to liberate them and place them in a condition where, as a matter of necessity, they would soon degenerate into the same barbarous condition as the present race in Africa; and that, too, when nine-tenths of American slaves are far better situated, and better provided for by their owners, than the abolitionists of the North are, who so kindly pretend to sympathize with them; and would spurn the offer, if it was proposed that they should change places with them.

In Dahoma, and a few other kingdoms in Africa, near the sea-coast, where the slavers have frequently visited the blacks, some of them wear clothes, which they procure from traders along on the coast, but even there they are badly clad; an American master would be indicted before the courts of the country, if he did not clothe his negroes better than the best of them, even on the coast, where they so frequently mingle with the whites; many of them have no other covering than a breech-clout around their hips to hide their nakedness, made of coarse cloth, or skins of wild beasts, while far in the interior, where they have not so many advantages, many of them go naked entirely, if we credit the accounts given by respectable travelers who have ventured far into the interior, and have given us descriptions of the manners and habits of the people in the interior. Bowen, who spent many years in Africa, and penetrated far into the interior, describes the Africans as going entirely naked in some places, and in others, with nothing more than a breech-clout and wrapper to hide their nakedness.

The whole country of Africa is governed by petty kings, who rule with absolute despotism as far as their jurisdiction extends; their voice is the law, and they frequently put their subjects to death, merely for the purpose of showing their authority. These kings frequently get at variance one with another, and go to war, and in such cases they are like other savages: they carry on a war of extermination, kill all they come to—men, women, and children, and eat one another for food, unless they can have a chance of selling their prisoners to a slaver; in that case, they spare their prisoners and barter them for goods. These tribes, some two or more, are continually at war with each other, and it is seldom or never the case that the whole country is at peace; in this way, at times, whole provinces are laid waste, and the inhabitants entirely destroyed; repeopled again, and again destroyed at another remote period; and there is but little prospect of affairs ever being much better, until the country is conquered by some civilized nation, and the whole of the natives enslaved and put to work as the American negroes now are. Then, and not until then, will Africa be at peace, and her natives become civilized, useful, and happy. The natives are very fond of dancing, and Bowen describes them as putting on a

WILD AFRICANS ROASTING ONE OF THEIR NUMBER.

great many awkward airs and gestures in that kind of exercise, and those who can place themselves in the most numerous and awkward positions are considered the best dancers. Their houses are little huts made of mud and sticks, rudely constructed, and often no other furniture than a few leaves and some grass on the dirt floor as a bed, and a pot to boil their food in, among the most civilized, while at other places they live in caves or hollow trees, and eat their food raw like the hogs. In the northern part of Africa, there is a small race of people called Earthmans, about three feet high; they live in the ground and burrow like rabbits, go entirely naked, and are unable to contend against the larger race; the consequence is, that whenever a large African meets with an Earthman, he never fails to butcher him and make soup of his carcass; they will kill an Earthman and eat him with as little compunction of conscience as an American negro would kill an opossum, and do it with as much sport.

As little is yet known of Africa as any country on the globe by civilized man; the country has never as yet been entirely traversed by any traveler, and there is no doubt but there are many other petty kingdoms and despotisms within its borders, of which there has never yet been any account given to the world. Tagard, in his travels, ventured several hundred miles into the interior, and visited many of their petty kings, but has never explored the extreme northern regions; as did also Bowen, who spent several years among them as a missionary, and visited Zoruba, Mahony, Monrovia, and many other provinces, of which they have given us some accounts; but of the far northern regions they can tell us nothing, and they yet remain to be explored. There is no doubt but that it has frequently been attempted to be explored, and the travelers were captured and eaten by the natives. Some of the tribes of Africa are Mohammedans, and acquired their religion no doubt by their frequent intercourse with the Arabs; but many of them are idolators, and worship idols, and we have accounts given by travelers in Africa of some of the tribes there worshiping the devil.

The country in Africa abounds with fruits of various description, which grow wild in the woods, and constitute a principal part of the food of the natives. The cocoa-nut grows wild in many places, also the pineapple, and the plantain, and the yam: upon such food they exist and feed. In some places they cultivate the pinder, or ground peas, and the yam; this they roast, or boil in a pot. The yam is a favorite dish with all classes, and the country produces it in abundance, and it is cultivated for the purpose; the woods abound also in monkeys in great abundance, and the African is very fond of their flesh.

Such is the condition of the negro race in a free state in Africa; they are never safe, always exposed, either to the cruel tyranny of their kings, the ferocity of their savage and blood-thirsty neighbors, or the ravages of famine; are destitute of every necessary of life, entire strangers to luxuries, void of the knowledge of the true religion of Jesus Christ, and sunk into the lowest state of idolatry and degradation.

While, on the other hand, take a view of the American negro on his master's plantation: we find him well clothed to suit every season of the year, with comfortable clothes for his body, and shoes for his feet; we enter his habitation, and there we find he has a comfortable, neat habitation to protect him from the weather, a comfortable mattress or bed on which to rest his head when tired or fatigued, with every comfort for his support. We find him intelligent and contented; he can converse on the subject of the Christian religion with heart-felt piety, and in many cases point to the time of being at some preaching where a white man had preached, when he was converted, and felt the saving grace of the Lord Jesus Christ shed abroad in his soul. He rises early in the morning, puts on his clothes, goes whistling and happily to his work; by his labor, fields are cleared, fences made; corn, wheat, potatoes, cotton, and every variety of valuable plants and seeds are produced in abundance; by his labor, the iron ore is dug up out of the earth, and the railroads are graded, steam saw-mills are kept at work, and cotton furnished for every civilized nation in the world; and he glories in beholding the earth yielding her fruits in abundance from the effect of his labor. He rests secure under the protection

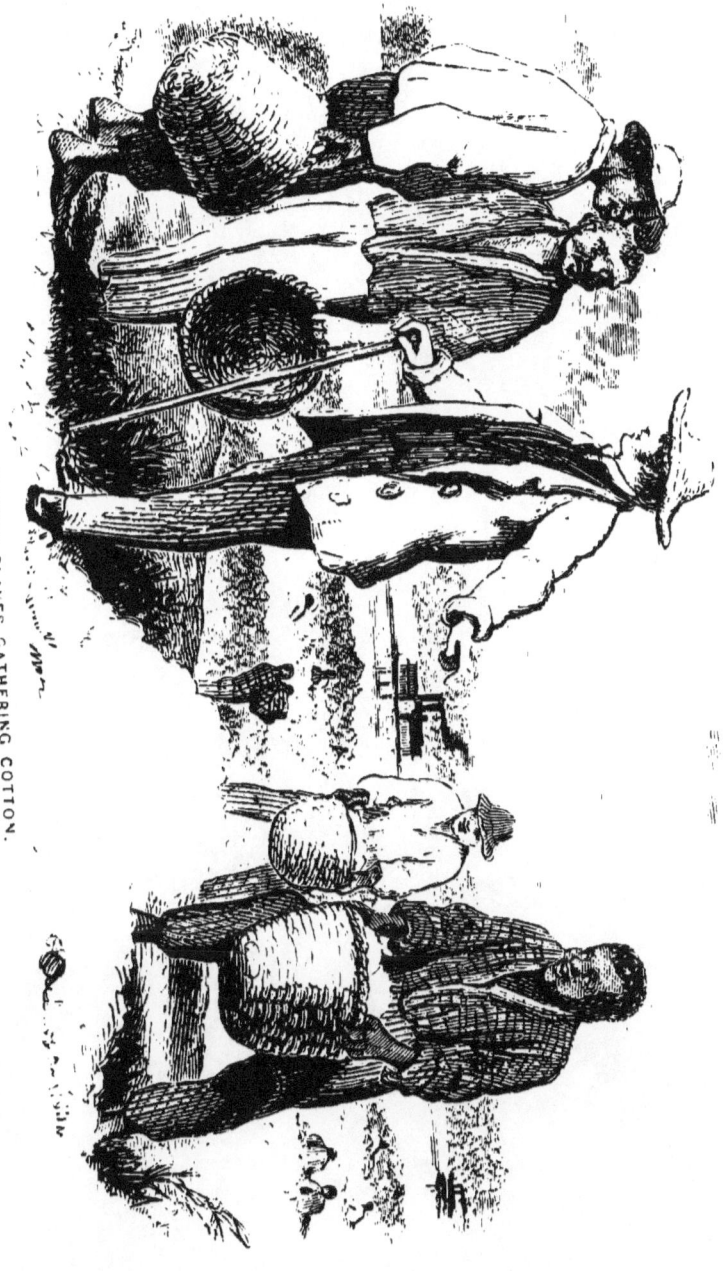

AMERICAN SLAVES GATHERING COTTON.

of his master, and is never afraid of being eaten by his neighbors; he is no idolator or Mohammedan; he has no use for idols, but worships his God, and acknowledges Jesus Christ as his Saviour. They generally have a plenty to eat, a plenty to wear, and a plenty to do, and with this they are satisfied and apparently the best contented and happiest people in the world.

But some will say, your slaveholders in the United States sometimes use their slaves cruel, and sometimes kill them; how can all this happen, if your slaves are the happiest people in the world? To this I answer, that sometimes a slave is killed, but it is generally a matter of necessity, in order to control them; that sometimes there are some so very bad that their owners are compelled to kill them. But, after all, there are not one-half as many slaves killed by white men in the slave-holding States as there are white men killed by one another in the same States, or in the non-slaveholding States, in proportion to numbers; and in all the slave States put together there are not as many negroes killed annually, by white men, as are butchered by a single African king in his petty dominion: not one-tenth as many as are killed by Great Britain, in sending her subjects to be slaves in the wars; or France, or Spain, or any other nation. And as to cruelty, a master is not allowed to inflict any cruel or unusual ill-treatment on his slave by the laws of the country, and if he does so, he is liable to be indicted and punished; and we more frequently hear of cruel and unusual ill-treatment in the non-slaveholding States inflicted by white people on each other, than we do in the slaveholding States on slaves. The slaves are protected by the laws of the country and their owners, and it is to the interest of the slaveholder to see that his slaves are properly treated; and it is very rarely the case that a slaveholder ever unnecessarily abuses his slaves, or permits it to be done by others.

CHAPTER V.

The Probable Result as to Universal Slavery of the African Race.—All Civilized Nations would be benefited by having them as Slaves.—Their Probable Destiny.—The Destruction of the English Possessions in the West Indies by Freeing their Slaves.—Evil Result of Freeing the Slaves in San Domingo.

Taking it for granted, then, that the African race was intended, from the beginning, to be slaves; that their physical and mental organization are so constructed as to fit them for that condition; that they are the only people in the world who will submit to be kept in bondage by their own color, and men of every other nation, whether they are in the ascendency in numbers or not; that a state of slavery is the only one in which the black man can exist as a moral and an intelligent human being; that it is in that condition alone he is capable of being of any service, either to himself or the balance of mankind; and that in that condition he is as useful, or more so, than any other class of human beings, both to himself and the rest of mankind; that it is in that condition alone he is by any means happy or contented; and that by his peculiar organization, he prefers to be a slave to being free,—we can come to but one conclusion as to the final destiny of the whole African race, and that is, that they will eventually all be slaves; that the whole race of the descendants of Ham will eventually be brought under that curse which was pronounced by Noah, shortly after the flood, on Ham, for his wickedness and his disobedience, that he should be a servant of servants; that the descendants of Shem and Japheth, when they shall find that all of their efforts to raise the descendants of their brother Ham in the scale of human beings, from their present degraded and vile condition in a state of freedom, shall fail; when they shall be brought to see that they have invariably pursued the wrong course in trying to civilize Africa as she is, and that all of their efforts will be vain; that the only condition in which the sons of Ham are at all happy, contented, civilized, and useful, is in a state of slavery, for which they were intended; that a state of slavery is the only one in which they will thrive and prosper; and that, in that state, they are capable of civilization and being Christianized, and are capable, in an eminent degree, of aiding and assisting in the support of themselves, and adding much to the common stock for the benefit of the whole,—they will bring them all to a state of bondage, and place them under masters and overseers, that they may fulfill the purpose for which they are so well qualified and seem to be designed; that England, France, Russia, Prussia, Austria, the whole of the United States, and every civilized nation in the world, will have the African as a slave; that they would enslave them as a matter of benevolence, if nothing more, seeing that they cannot exist in any other condition as civilized human beings. They may experiment for awhile, by continuing to liberate those who are in a state of bondage, from a false notion of Christian duty; but when they find that by thus setting them free, they destroy whole continents, by laying waste a country which has been kept in cultivation by slave labor; that they destroy the commerce of the world, and break down the manufacturing interest everywhere, and reduce the slave, from a condition of plenty and protection, to a state of starvation and degradation; that in trying to free the slave, they are bringing a curse upon him, and on themselves, and fighting against the immutable decrees of God,—they will then turn and pursue the only proper course to effect the object which many of the abolitionists now pretend to have in view, to raise the African in the scale of human beings, and teach them the Christian religion, by bringing all those who are in a wild state of freedom into bondage. Suppose, for a moment, that the three and a half millions of slaves now in the United States were set free, what would be the effect of such a course on the United States and the rest of the world? The consequence would be, that every cotton factory in the world would stop operations, and not less than one hundred thousand white persons in Europe and the United States, who are engaged in the manufacturing of cotton goods, be thrown out of employment; the whole of the Southern slaveholding States would be left barren and uncultivated, and instead of exporting upwards of three hundred millions of dollars' worth of exports into foreign countries, and importing as much in return, as they now do, they would not export one dollar's worth. The shipping interest would feel the effect, and dwindle away for the want of freights; for the want of custom-house duties, the government would have to resort to direct taxation to make up the deficiencies, and thus indirectly enslave the white people in all of the non-slaveholding States, in order to liberate the blacks, who, to make the best of it, would only be as so many drones in the hive, who would have to be supported by the whites. But this is not all; the whites and the blacks can never exist together in any country in a state of equality: a murderous, exterminating war would commence immediately, in the which one party or the other would soon be exterminated and killed off. If the whites should kill off the blacks, they would do nothing more in the slaveholding States than barely to make a support; the climate is such that white men cannot cultivate the soil to much advantage, while the negro is admirably adapted to it. If the negroes should succeed, there would soon be a country of black savages, in a few generations, as barbarous and degraded as the wild Africans now in Africa; and all of this beautiful country, now in a high state of cultivation, on the sea-board, in the slaveholding States, rendered useless to all the world, and left a barren waste, to be inhabited by a set of wild, black, cannibal barbarians, who would be ever and anon a pest to the border white States, far more terrible than any ancient Indian tribe. Of the proceeds of slave labor in the fourteen slaveholding States of the United States, there is now exported about three hundred millions of dollars' worth annually, and there is about twice as much kept at home, for home consumption, which would make, as the probable estimate of the whole amount of slave labor in the United States, at about nine hundred millions of dollars' worth, an estimate of more than one-half of the entire production of the whole nation; an item greatly to be considered in the annals of national importance.

Just see what the result was, in the Island

of San Domingo, when the French government declared the slaves of that island to be free; the consequence was, that instead of showing themselves grateful for the favor the government had done them, they immediately exterminated the whites, and France lost her possession of the island entirely, and the blacks set up a government of their own, under which they were more persecuted than under the government of their former masters; and, although it has not been sixty years since the occurrence, the blacks have since greatly degenerated in their morals and civilization, and, in the course of one century more, will be in as bad a state of barbarism and savage ignorance as the inhabitants of Africa, unless again enslaved by some civilized nation. Look at the British possessions in the West Indies, where a few years ago their islands flourished and prospered as the rose, under the influence of African slave labor; and now, since they have liberated their slaves, within a few years past, their islands are valueless and a dead expense to the nation, and the negro population in a far worse condition than before.

The Parliament of Great Britain, in A.D. 1832, liberated her African slaves, and appropriated out of the public treasury £21,000,000, which is equivalent to $105,000,000, to indemnify the owners of the slaves. For the success of this experiment, Professor Josiah Priest, A.M., and member of the Antiquarian Society of New York, says, in his valuable work on "Bible Evidence of Slavery," that a recent letter from Jamaica states, that the poverty and industrial prostration of the island are almost incredible; it says that, since 1833, out of six hundred and fifty sugar estates then in cultivation, more than one hundred and fifty have been abandoned, and the works broken up; this has thrown out of cultivation over 200,000 acres of rich land, which, in 1832, gave employment to about 30,000 laborers, and yielded over 15,000 hogsheads of sugar and 6000 puncheons of rum. During the same period, over 500 coffee plantations have been abandoned, and their works broken up; this threw out of cultivation over 200,000 acres more of land, which in 1832 required the labor of over 30,000 men. These experiments show very clearly the great evils which result from liberating the African from his state of bondage to the white race. Is there any man, with a single spark of Christian feeling within his breast, who would desire to see the black slaves of the United States set free, with all these lights before his eyes, when the inevitable consequence would be extermination of the whole race in the end, and the massacre of thousands of the white population in the bloody controversy which would ensue; a stoppage to the manufacturing interest in cotton goods all over the world, and a complete overthrow of commerce in every civilized nation? Those who would desire such a scene, are surely blind to observation, reason, and revelation, or else, like Beelzebub, are enemies to the whole human race.

CHAPTER VI.

The People of the Slave States, of all others, have a right to own their Slaves.—Slavery introduced by Great Britain and France into the United States.—Judicial Decisions by the Courts of Great Britain and the United States on the Subject of African Slavery.

The thirteen colonies which, on the 4th day of July, A.D. 1776, asserted their independence, were governed by British laws. Our ancestors, in their emigration to this country, brought with them the common law of England as their birthright; they adopted its principles for their government as far as it was not incompatible with the peculiarities of their situation, in a rude and unsettled country. Great Britain, then, having the sovereignty over them, possessed the power to regulate their institutions. to control their commerce, and give laws to their intercourse with all the nations of the earth. Great Britain thus exercising sovereign power of the thirteen colonies, did establish slavery in them; did maintain and protect the institution; did carry on, foster, and support the African slave-trade, and forbade the colonies permission, either to emancipate or export their slaves, and forbade them from inaugurating any legislation in diminishing or discouraging the institution.

The first permanent settlement made on this continent by the English, was made under a charter granted in A.D. 1606, in the fourth year of James I., to Sir Thomas Gates and his associates. A few unsuccessful attempts had previously been made by others, but the first permanent settlement made under the authority of the Crown was made in 1606. That charter was superseded by a *quo warranto*, issued at the instance of the British Crown; and in A.D. 1620, another charter was granted to the Duke of Lenox and his associates, who were incorporated under the name of the Plymouth Company: to that Company the coast was granted from the 40th to the 48th degree of north latitude. This charter was followed by successive grants to different noblemen and companies, until the entire coast was disposed of. In A.D. 1664, all the territory was granted to the Duke of York, as far south as Delaware Bay; and in 1663 and 1666, the entire coast, extending from the 29th degree of north latitude to that celebrated line of 36° 30' north, since so famous in the history of our intestine disputes, was granted to Lord Clarendon and his associates. Thus was conveyed the whole coast comprised within our present limits.

And before this very first settlement, the slave-trade had been inaugurated and established in Great Britain. The first historical notice we have of this fact, is the grant of a charter by Queen Elizabeth to a company formed for the purpose of supplying slaves to the Spanish American colonies; the queen herself was a shareholder. Subsequently, in A.D. 1662, under Charles II., a monopoly was created in favor of a company authorized to export to the colonies three thousand slaves per annum; and so valuable was this privilege considered, so great was the influence required for the purpose of obtaining a share in it, that it was placed under the auspices of the Queen Dowager and the Duke of York. The king himself, in order to encourage the traffic in African slaves, issued his proclamation, offering a bounty of a hundred acres of land to his subjects for every four slaves employed in the cultivation of it.

The merchants of London found their trade to the slave coast very much cramped by this royal monopoly, granted to favorites of the Crown, and they loudly complained that they were excluded from the advantages of so prosperous a traffic; and in A.D. 1695, in committee of the whole, the Commons of England

Resolved, That for the better supply of the plantations, all the subjects of Great Britain should have liberty to trade in Africa for negroes, with such limits as should be prescribed by Parliament.

In the 9th and 10th William III., an act was passed partially relaxing this monopoly, the preamble to which states—

That the trade was highly beneficial to the kingdom, and to the plantations and colonies thereto belonging.

This partial relaxation was unsatisfactory; petitions continued to pour in; in 1708, the Commons again

Resolved, That the trade was important,

and ought to be free and open to all the queen's subjects trading from Great Britain.

And in 1711, they again resolved that this trade ought to be free in a regulated company; the plantations ought to be supplied with negroes at reasonable rates; a considerable stock was necessary for carrying on the trade to the best advantage, and that an export of £100,000 at least, in merchandise, should be annually made from Great Britain to Africa. Finally, in the year A.D. 1749, these repeated resolutions of the Commons and petitions of the merchants of London accomplished the desired result. They gained their object by the passage of the act of 23d George II., throwing open the trade, and declaring the slave-trade to be very advantageous to Great Britain, and necessary for supplying the plantations and colonies thereunto belonging with a sufficient number of negroes at reasonable rates.

Thus we see, that Great Britain unhesitatingly went into the slave traffic in negroes by the wholesale; buying annually £100,000 worth of slaves, at prices in Africa, an amount nearly equivalent to a half million of dollars;

in which all classes were permitted to share the profits, from the monarch to the peasant, and was considered and so declared to be a very lucrative and profitable business, both to the government and the stockholders of individuals concerned; yet, notwithstanding all this, that the stockholders acquired millions by the trade, the African, who was sold in servitude, was the greatest gainer of all concerned: he was taken from a state of heathenish paganism, from a state of naked and savage barbarity, and placed in a condition where he would hear the gospel of Jesus Christ preached, to the salvation of his soul, and under a master who would restrict him in his criminal practices and teach him the morals of the Christian religion, clothe him and feed him as a rational being, and make him do such work as he could and ought to do for his own benefit and that of the rest of the human race; by which means the American slave has risen far above the common African in the wilds of Africa, in intelligence, morality, and religion.

This legislation of Great Britain fixed the institution upon the colonies; they had no power to resist it; they could only remonstrate and petition, and make attempts to legislate at home to diminish the evil, and every such attempt was sternly repressed by the British Crown.

In 1760, South Carolina passed an act prohibiting the further importation of African slaves. The act was rejected by the Crown; the governor was reprimanded, and a circular was sent to all the governors of the colonies, warning them against presuming to countenance such legislation.

In 1765, a similar bill was twice read in the Assembly of Jamaica. The news reached Great Britain before its final passage; instructions were sent to the royal governor; he called the House of Assembly before him, communicated his instructions, and forbade any further progress of the bill.

In 1774, in spite of this discountenancing the bill by Great Britain, two bills passed the Legislature of Jamaica; and the Earl of Dartmouth, then Secretary of State, wrote to Sir Basil Keith, the Governor of the colony, that these measures had created alarm to the merchants of Great Britain engaged in that branch of commerce, and forbidding him, on pain of removal from his office, to assent to such laws.

Finally, in 1775, mark the date, after the revolutionary struggle had commenced, while the Continental Congress was in session, after armies had been levied, after Crown Point and Ticonderoga had been taken possession of by the insurgent colonists, and after the first blood had been shed in the Revolution at Lexington, this same Earl of Dartmouth, in answer to a remonstrance from an agent of the colonies, replied: We cannot allow the colonies to check or discourage in any degree a traffic so beneficial to the nation.

Thus, down to the very commencement of the Revolution, which separated Great Britain from the thirteen colonies, African slavery was forced by her on the colonies, without their consent, regardless of their approbation, and may, therefore, be considered the common law of the land, ingrafted from the mother country.

And, if we will examine the decision of her judges, and the answers of her lawyers to questions propounded by the Crown and assembled bodies, we will find that slavery is recognized by the common law of England, and slaves are declared to be merchandise and property, and transferable the same as any other chattels.

A short time prior to the year 1713, a contract had been formed between Spain and a certain company called the Royal Guinea Company, that had been established in France. This contract was technically called in those days an *assiento*.

By the treaty of Utrecht, of the 11th of April, 1713, Great Britain, through her diplomatist, obtained a transfer of that contract—she yielded considerations for it—the obtaining of which was greeted in England with great joy; it was considered a triumph of diplomacy. It was followed, in the month of May, 1713, by a new contract in form, by which the British government undertook, for the term of thirty years then next to come, to transport annually 4800 slaves to the Spanish American colonies at a fixed price. Almost immediately after this new contract, a question arose in the English council as to the true legal character of the slaves thus to be transported to the Spanish American colonies; and, according to the forms of the British constitution, the question was submitted by the Crown in council to the twelve judges of England; and they answered in the following words, to wit: In pursuance of his Majesty's order in council, hereunto annexed, we do humbly certify our opinion to be, that negroes are merchandise.

Signed by Lord Chief Justice Holt, Judge Pollextin, and eight other judges of England. This was immediately after the treaty of Utrecht, in 1713. Very soon after this, the spirit of fanaticism began to obtain a foothold in England; and, although large numbers of slaves were owned in Great Britain, and were daily sold in the public Exchange in London, (see 2 Haggard's Report, page 105,) questions arose as to the rights of the owners to retain property in their slaves; and the merchants of London, alarmed, submitted the question to Sir Philip York, who afterward became Lord Hardwick, and to Lord Talbot, who was then the Solicitor and Attorney-General of the kingdom. The question was propounded to them: What are the rights of a British owner of a slave in England? And this is the answer of those two legal functionaries. They certified that a slave coming from the West Indies to England, with or without his master, does not become free, and his master's property in him is not thereby determined nor varied; and his master may legally compel him to return to the plantation.

And in A.D. 1749, the same question again came up before Sir Philip York, then Lord Chancellor of England, under the title of Lord Hardwick, and by a decree in Chancery in the case before him, he affirmed the doctrine which he had uttered when he was Attorney-General of Great Britain.

Such were the decisions of the judges of England up to A.D. 1771, when the spirit of fanaticism began greatly to prevail, by which Lord Mansfield was driven to a different decision in the celebrated Sommerset case; by which judicial legislation, we may term it, subverted the common law of England, and decided, not that a slave carried to England from the West Indies by his master thereby became free, but that by the law of England, if the slave resisted the master, there was no remedy by which the master could exercise his control; that the colonial legislation, which afforded the master means of controlling his property, had no authority in England; and that England, by her laws, had provided no substitute for that authority. To this decision Lord Mansfield was driven by the spirit of fanaticism; for he had no precedent or law on which to base it. On the contrary, both law and precedent were clearly against the decision; for he used every effort in his power to get the parties to compromise the case, so that he could evade giving a decision on the subject; but they would not compromise. But this decision of Lord Mansfield had but little effect on subsequent decisions of the English courts, and only went to tarnish his reputation and show his vacillating disposition. For, as late as A.D. 1827, twenty years after Great Britain had abolished the slave-trade, and six years before she confiscated the property of the colony, which she forced them to buy, the celebrated case of the slave Grace, well known to all lawyers, was brought before Lord Stowell, one of the most learned and firm judges in all the kingdom, in which it was decided quite different; it was contended in argument that the slave Grace, having been brought to England by her master, was free; that once she was free, she was always free. That the English atmosphere was too pure to be breathed by a slave. Lord Stowell, in answering that legal argument, said: That after painful and laborious research into historical records, he did not find anything touching the peculiar fitness of the English atmosphere for respiration, during the ten centuries that slaves had lived in England.

The point was also raised in this case, that slavery did not exist by common law usage anywhere, but was only the creature of positive legislation; and here is what Lord Stowell said on that point in the case, to wit: Having adverted to most of the objections that arise to the removal of slavery in the colonies, I have first to observe that it returns upon the slave by the same title by which it grew up; originally it never was in antiquia a creature of law, but of that custom which operates with the force of law; and when it is cried out that *malus usus abolendus est*, it is first to be proven that even in the consideration of England the use of slavery is considered as a *malus usus* in the colonies. Is that a *malus usus* which the court of kings, privy council, and the courts of chancery are every day carrying into full effect in all considerations of property; in the one by appeal, and in the other by original causes; and all this enjoined and confirmed by statutes? Still less is it to be considered as a *malus usus* in the colonies themselves, where it has been incorporated into full life and establishment, where it is the system of the State, and of every individual in it; and fifty years have passed without any authorized condemnation of it in England as a *malus usus* in the colonies. And this was fifty years after Lord Mansfield's speech in the Sommerset case.

The fact is, that in England, where villeinage of both sorts went into total decay, we had communication with no other country, and, therefore, it is triumphantly declared, as I have before observed, once a freeman, ever a freeman; there being no other country with which we had immediate connection, which at the time of suppressing that system we had any occasion to trouble ourselves about; but slavery was a very great source of the mercantile interest of the country, and was on that account largely considered by the mother country as a great source of its wealth and strength. Treaties were made on that account, and the colonies compelled to submit to those treaties by the authority of this country. This system continued entire; instead of being condemned as *malus usus*, it was regarded as a most eminent source of its riches and power. It was at a late period of the last century that it was condemned in England as an institution not fit to exist here, for reasons peculiar to our own condition; but it has been continued in our colonies, favored and supported by our own courts, which have liberally imparted to it their protection and encouragement. To such a system, while it is supported, I rather feel it to be too strong to apply the maxim *malus usus abolendus est*. The time may come when this institution may fall, in the colonies, as other institutions have done in other flourishing countries; but I am of opinion it can only be effected at the joint expense of both countries; for it is in a peculiar manner the crime of this country, and I rather feel it to be an objection to this species of emancipation; that it is indeed to be a very cheap measure, hereby throwing the whole expense upon the country. (2 Haggard's Reports, page 128, *et seq.*)

Such was the opinion of Lord Stowell in the celebrated case of the slave Grace. At the time of his decision, he was in correspondence with Judge Story, a man of known ability and patriotism; and he wrote to Judge Story upon the subject of his opinion, who was asked to consider it, and give his opinion about it; and here is an extract from his answer, to wit: I have read with great attention your judgment in the slave case. Upon the fullest consideration which I have been able to give the subject, I entirely concur in your views; if I had been called upon to pronounce a judgment in a like case, I should certainly have arrived at the same conclusion. That was the opinion of Judge Story, given in this case, in A.D. 1827.

These facts, supported by the decisions of

such men as Lord Stowell and Judge Story, ought to be sufficient to convince any unprejudiced mind that slavery exists in the United States by the common law brought from England, and existed in all of the English colonies in the same way; and that it existed in England by the same usage until very recently. But, in looking still further, we see that it is the common law of the whole continent, both North and South America alike.

The European powers which joined and co-operated with Great Britain in the discovery and establishing of colonies on this continent, all followed the same views of policy. France, Spain, Portugal, and England occupied the whole continent north and south; the legislation of all of them was the same. Louis XIII., by royal edict, established slavery in all his colonies in America; and, through the interference of Lascasas, the Spanish Crown inaugurated the slave-trade with a view of substituting the servile labor of the African for that of the Indians, who had been reduced to slavery by their Spanish conquerors. As regards Portugal, she inaugurated the trade; she originally supplied all the colonies; and the empire of Brazil to-day, with its servile labor, is the legitimate fruit of the colonial policy of the Portuguese government in the sixteenth century. She began her trade in 1508; some authors say even before the colonization of America in the fifteenth century.

Slavery was thus the recognized institution, both of the Old and New World. White slavery existed in England until comparatively a recent date; it did not finally disappear until the reign of James II. The system of villeinage, of which all the law writers speak, was a system of slavery in its strictest sense. Villeins were all slaves, as much so as the negroes now are in America. There were two kinds: villeins regardant, and villeins in gross; and the only difference between them was that the villeins regardant were attached to the soil, and could not be sold away from the glebe; they followed the conveyance of the estate in the hands of the lord. But the villeins in gross were chattels, sold from hand to hand just as negroes or cattle, or any other species of property are now sold — a concise account of which is given in the first volume of the celebrated treatise of Mr. Spence on the Equity Jurisdiction of the Courts of Chancery. That volume contains an admirable, concise history of the English law; some statements are contained therein relative to the English law of villeinage, as also in Mr. Blackstone's Commentaries on the Laws of England. But a true and fair picture of the state of villeinage in England is very concisely portrayed in the celebrated argument of Mr. Hargrave, the great lawyer, who was the counsel for the slave in the Sommerset case; one passage will give us an idea of what the villein was, under the common law of England. He said: The condition of the villein had most of the incidents which I have before described, in giving the idea of slavery in general. His service was uncertain and indeterminate, such as his lord saw fit to require; or, as some of our ancient writers express it, he knew not in the evening what he was to do in the morning. He was bound to do whatever he was commanded; he was liable to beating, imprisonment, or any other species of chastisement his lord might prescribe, except killing and maiming. He was incapable of acquiring property for his own benefit, the rule being *quo quid acquiritur servo acquiritur domino.* He was himself the subject of property, as such salable and transmissible; if he was a villein regardant, he passed with the manor or land to which he was annexed, but might be severed at the pleasure of the lord. If he was a villein in gross, he was a hereditament or a chattel real, according to his lord's interest, being descendable to the heir where the lord was absolute owner, and transmissible to the executor where the lord had only a term of years in him. Lastly, the slavery extended to the issue; if both parents were villeins, or if the father was a villein—our law deriving the condition of the child from that of the father, contrary to the Roman law, in which the rule was *partus sequiter ventrem.*

The origin of villeinage is principally to be derived from the wars between the British, Saxons, Danish, and Norman ancestors, while they were contending for the possession of the country. Judge Fitzherbert, in his reading on the fourth of Edward I. stat. i., entitled *extenta manerii,* supposes villeinage to have commenced at the Conquest, by the distribution then made of the forfeited lands, and of the vanquished inhabitants resident upon them; but there were many bondmen in England before the Conquest, as appears by the Anglo-Saxon laws regulating them; and, therefore, it would be nearer the truth to attribute the origin of villeins, as well to the preceding wars and revolutions in this country, as to the effects of this Conquest. (20th Howell's State Trials, pp. 36, 37.)

White slavery in England was protected by the common law, down to James II., and its disappearance was gradual. The monarchs themselves held a property in them; and when they were liberated, they had to pay a full equivalent for their freedom. Queen Elizabeth. during her reign, issued a commission to Cecil, Lord Burleigh. and Sir William Mildmay, giving them authority to go into her counties of Gloucester, Cornwall. Devon, and Sommerset. and there to manumit her slaves, by getting from them a reasonable price for their liberty. That is the way slavery was abolished in England; it was abolished by the gradual emancipation of the slaves, resulting from the sale of the lord to the slave himself of his right over him. Here is a copy of the commission, which may be found in the Appendix to the 20th volume of Howell's State Trials, which reads as follows:—

Elizabeth, by the grace of God, etc., to our right trustie and well beloved Councillor, Sir W. Cecil, of the Garter, Knighte, Lord Burghley, and Highe Treasurer of England, and to our trustie and right well beloved Councillor, Sir Walter Mildmay, Knighte, Chancellor and Under Treasurer of our Exchequer, Greetinge: Whereas divers and sundrie of our poore, faithful, and loyal subjects, being borne, bounde in blode, and regardant to divers and sundrie our manors and possessions, within our realm of England, have made humble suyte unto us to be manumised, enfranchised, and made free, with theire children and sequels, by reason whereof, they, theire children, and sequels may become more apt and fitte members for the service of us and of our commonwealth; we, then, having tender considerations of theire said suyte, and well considering the same to be acceptable to Almightie God.

Now, we would suppose she was going to give them their liberty. Not at all; but, kind queen as she is, willing to sell them to themselves at a fair price, like one negro would sell a quart of pinders to another, for its full value! What merciful kindness! And so she goes on:—

And we do committ and give unto you full power and authoritie by these presents to accept, admitte, and receive to be manumised, enfranchised, and made free, such and so many of our bondmen and bond-women in blode, with all and every theire children and sequells, theire goodes, landes, tenementes, and hereditaments as are now apperteynynge or regarduante to all or any of our manors, landes, tenementes, possessions or hereditaments within the said several counties of Cornwall, Devon, Sommerset, and Gloucester, as to you, by your discressions shall seme mete and convenient. Compoundinge with them for such reasonable fines or sommes of money to be taken and received to our use, for manumyssion and enfranchisement; and for the possessions and enjoying of all and singular theire landes, tenementes, hereditaments, goodes, and chattels, whatsoever as you and they can agree, for the same after your wisdomes and discressions.

Here, then, was slavery in its widest and broadest acceptation in Great Britain, in the time of Elizabeth; and it never finally disappeared from the kingdom until the reign of James II.

In France, they had also a system of white slaves of the same kind; there they were called *gens de maine morte,* most main people, because they belonged to the estates; and they were not liberated until 1779, long after black slaves were introduced into the French possessions in America. They were enfranchised by a royal edict, commencing in these words:—

We have been greatly affected by the consideration that a large number of our subjects, still attached as slaves to the glebe, are regarded as forming a part of it, as it were; that, deprived of the liberty of their persons, and of the rights of property, they themselves are considered as the property of their lords; that they have not the consolation of bequeathing of their goods; and that, except in a few cases rigorously circumscribed, they cannot even transmit to their own children the fruits of their own labor.

Thus fell the last remnant of white slavery in France, in 1779; after the independence of the United States, and after it was ascertained that the negro race were much better adapted to slavery than the white.

That slavery of the black population is the common law of the land, and is so recognized, every one of the slaveholding States of the thirteen States, at the time of the Declaration of Independence, who afterwards abolished slavery, found it necessary to do so by positive statute to that effect. There was no law of the colonies establishing African slavery previous to that date, and it therefore existed by the common law of the country, brought from the mother country; and to abolish it required a direct statute.

Those States which abolished slavery did not do so all of a sudden, but gradually; giving time in all cases for the owners to send them to the Southern slaveholding States, to sell them for a fair price, which they did by thousands, pocketed the money, returned home with the proceeds, and then raised a great hue and cry, that African slavery in the United States was abominable! What very sympathetic philanthropists these Northern negro-speculators are!—they would sell their grandmother for money to the Southern planter, then weep over the evils of slavery! The States which liberated their slaves were not the losers; their citizens sent off their slaves, and sold them in the Southern States, where they are now faring much better than many of their former owners are in the free States: better fed, better clothed, and better satisfied with their condition.

The Constitution of the United States recognizes African slavery, and guarantees a protection to the owners of the same, in every part of the nation. The free States are bound by that instrument to protect the slaveholder in the possession and enjoyment of his slave-property; and whenever they fail to do it, they violate that sacred instrument, which binds the States together as a band of brothers; which makes them formidable and respected, both at home and abroad. In addition to the express recital in the Constitution of the United States, guaranteeing to the owner of slaves protection to their property in every State in the Union, in order to dispel all doubt on the subject, the Supreme Court of the United States, the highest judicial tribunal in the world, has clearly decided the question, in the celebrated Dred Scott case, which was commenced before the United States District Court in the State of Missouri, in November, 1853, and carried up by writ of error to the Supreme Court of the nation, where it was decided by the Supreme Court: That negroes were slaves in the United States, and the property still continued in the owner, whether in a free State or a slaveholding State; and that the slave Dred Scott was not entitled to his freedom; that slaves were not citizens of the United States, but property, which vested in their owners.

The opinion of the Supreme Court was delivered by Chief Justice Taney, one of the greatest jurists, and most upright and impartial judges the world has ever known.

With all these facts before us, then, it is evident, beyond all doubt, that African slavery in the United States is the common law of the land; that it exists without any legislative statute to support it; and that whenever the United States acquired any new territory, the slaveholder had an undoubted right to take his slave-property to it, as he had any other kind; and it is the bounden duty of the Government of the United States, and every State in the Union, whether slaveholding or not, to protect him in the enjoyment of his property. They have agreed to do so in their compact: the Constitution under which they exist as one great and formidable government requires it; the interest of all demands it; and every just man and patriot, and obeying man, who has any love for his country, or any desire for the perpetuity of the union of the States, or any regard or feeling for the negroes themselves, or any feeling of humanity for his own race, should desire it. All should unite in the mutual protection of each other, and of each other's rights, in any and every species of property whatever. If they will do this, and let every State make her own regulation about her slave-property, as well as all other species of goods and chattels, and never permit the subject ever once to be agitated before the Congress of the nation, this great republic will very soon be the Eden of the earth; its influence will extend to the remotest parts of the world; and, in point of strength and population, will be equal to all the world besides. As Mr. Webster observed, a few years ago, in Congress: That the child was now born who would live to see our nation possessed of one hundred millions of inhabitants, if our States would only remain united. Then, what it would be in the course of three centuries to come, we can scarcely calculate. We may safely suggest, that it would amount to more than a million of millions of people; that the whole continent of North America and South America, with every island within its range, will belong to this great republic, every one in their proper place, for which they were designed— the whites all free, and the negroes all slaves; each contributing, according to his capacity, largely for the benefit of the whole. A powerful republic, governed by the freemen of the land, with no king but God, our creator and preserver, who rules directly, and governs all according to his own good pleasure; to whom be all the glory, power, and honor, now and forever more.

What would be said of the Southern people in the slaveholding States, if they should take their horses to the free States and sell them, and they should run away and return, and the owners should come after their property, and the people of the slaveholding States should say to them, You shall not take your property back; they have crossed the line, and got into our State, and you shall not take them away? They would be looked upon as thieves and robbers, and every act of the kind would loosen the bands which bind them together, and their union could last but a little while; instead of safety and protection from the union, it would only amount to robbery and fraud. So, the principle is just the same, if a slaveholder's slave runs away, and goes into a free State, and the citizens of the free State refuse to give him up to his owner; it is depriving the owner of his slave, and defrauding him of his property, and converting the union of the States into fraud and oppression, instead of safety and protection.

We say to the people of the free-soil States, You are our brothers; we constitute one great national family; we all have conceded certain rights to the general government for the protection and benefit of the whole; and other certain rights we have reserved to ourselves; among which reserved rights is the regulation of the subject of African slavery within our own borders. We are well convinced that in union there is strength; for Jesus Christ, the great Saviour of mankind, has taught us this lesson, which is handed down to us in the Holy Bible, wherein he says that a house divided against itself cannot stand; that a nation divided against itself cannot stand; and even that if Satan is divided in his kingdom that cannot stand.

That we wish to carry out our contract, as expressed in the Constitution of the United States, in its strictest sense; that we will give you permission to bring your property among us, let it be of what kind it may; that we will take up arms to fight against any nation on the earth who will dare to rob you of your property, either on the land or on the seas; that whenever the United States acquires any new territory, it shall be the common property of us all; and we will all take our property there, if we choose, whether it be slaves, dry goods, horses, cattle, or any other kind; and we will mutually join in the protection of each other, in the possession of that property; and when we see each other's property going astray, we will go according to the doctrines of the Bible: we will take it up and return it to our neighbor, to whom it of right belongs; that we will protect you in your rights, and in return you must protect us in our rights; there shall be no sectional divisions among us; there shall be no Northern, Southern, Eastern, or Western line of division among us; but we will all be as citizens of one great nation, and the interest of one of us shall be the interest of us all. When your property goes astray, and comes among us, we will not only deliver it up to you, when you come after it, but we will turn out en masse, and help you hunt it up; and you shall be assisted in obtaining it again; and if any man shall steal your property, and bring it among us, we will use every means in our power to ferret him out, and aid in delivering up to you both your property and the thief who stole it. Our land shall not be polluted as being the hiding place for thieves and stolen property. It shall be no place of refuge for any such.

And you in return must aid us in the same way: if our negroes run away and go among you, catch them, and return them to their proper owner. If any person should steal them, and carry them away, you use every exertion in your power to return the slave to his master, and deliver up the thief to be punished; and in this manner, a brotherly feeling will spring up among us, which will defy all the nations of the earth to sever us. We shall very soon hear nothing more of any slave running away from his master, to make his way to a free State, or of any man stealing slaves for any such purpose. Contention and disputes will soon cease among us; and instead of fighting against each other, and striving to injure one another, we shall all be striving to promote each other's welfare; and in doing that, promote our own. And if at any time any of you should so desire it, and wish to set any of our negroes free, as a matter of kindness on your part, just bring us the money, a fair valuation for the slave, and the owner will sell them to you at a fair price, and permit you to take them to a free State, and settle them there, if you like it; but we cannot permit free negroes to settle in among us; it would be unsafe and contrary to our policy, and calculated to breed disaffection and insurrection among our slaves. But if you will pay us the cash for them, you shall be at liberty to take them home with you, or send them where you please, where their influence will not tarnish the rest of our slaves; and by pursuing a policy of this kind, our nation will be bound to grow and flourish above every other on the earth, until it shall govern every other by its influence. It will not be necessary for us to take up arms to acquire territory; one by one, will every other government of the New World apply to our government for admittance, and beg to be received as a member of the Confederacy,

10*

until the whole continent shall become one great republic by special favor, most graciously granted, instead of compulsion by the sword; for it is such, and only such as would be anxious to be admitted, who would make worthy members of a great and growing republic like ours.

We have no use for friends and connections that we have to make such at the point of the bayonet; such do not possess the necessary cement to unite them to us in the capacity in which we ought to live; we want such as come willingly and anxiously, not so much for our benefit as for their own welfare and particular good. Such as come willingly are only such as are qualified to form sister States with us; on whom we can in safety rely in peace and in war. Our happy condition as a nation will be observed; and when other nations are broken up and destroyed by intestine wars, and trampled under foot by their powerful neighbors; when individual life, property, and liberty are continually in danger, and exposed to destruction in other countries, it will only be to become a member of this great republic to be safe, quiet, and protected; and other nations will, one by one, seek that refuge, by being united to our government, which they nowhere else can find.

Now, in A.D. 1860, the government of the United States is composed of thirty-four States, many of them larger than some of the kingdoms of Europe, and has, besides, territory sufficient to form some twenty more States, either of which, except the State of Delaware, is more powerful than any other government on the whole continent of North and South America, except Mexico, which no doubt will shortly be ingrafted into our Union, if we are willing to receive her; and a population of about thirty millions, rapidly increasing. It has increased since 1776, the date of the Declaration of Independence, from three millions of inhabitants, up to the present population of about thirty millions, and is now increasing much faster than ever. It is in this happy republic that all free-born white men are equal, and the poorest peasant has a chance, according to his merit, to rise to eminence, and fill the highest position in the country, equal with him who floats in wealth and splendor. It is in this republic that the power of steam was discovered by Robert Fulton, an American mechanic, not sixty years ago, which is now doing so much to enrich and civilize the world. It was in this republic that the existence of electricity was discovered by Dr. Benjamin Franklin, an American citizen, a discovery which is now astonishing the world, and conveying news on the lightning's wing from one State to another, a distance of thousands of miles in a few seconds. Though yet in its infancy, the world has never seen the day before, when any government has ever grown and prospered as has done the United States of North America, or a generation in which the arts and sciences have flourished as much as the present; or a nation whose arms were attended with more success in battling against their enemies;—all goes clearly to show that God, who rules the universe and guides the distinguished men and nations, has planted our government, directed its institutions, nurtured it with his hands, and governed its armies in battle.

Just look at the character of Washington, that great American general, who commanded the American army in the days of the Revolution—a character pure and unspotted, the envy of kings, a noted landmark, a disposition which seems to be different from that of any other man, a devoted follower of the Lord Jesus Christ, and a large African slaveholder; a man who, having liberated his country, resigned its crown, and we will see at once that he was a special character, created and placed in the situation he was destined to occupy for the purpose of achieving a certain object: his chief aim was the good of his country. Look again at the great military chieftains, whose reputation has shined as stars in the heaven, who succeeded him: Andrew Jackson, Zachary Taylor, John A. Quitman, Winfield Scott, and Sam Houston; great generals, wise statesmen, and pure patriots, all large African slaveholders; men in whose hands we might at any time risk the reins of our government in safety, guided and directed by the great Creator of the universe. Their characters stand as monuments of military greatness, bestowed upon the people of this nation for their protection. And also in the councils of our nation; look at the gigantic intellect of Henry Clay, Daniel

Webster, John C. Calhoun, James Buchanan, William Henry Harrison, Thomas Jefferson, and James Monroe, and the many other able statesmen who figured not long since in the councils of our nation, most of whom are now laid low in the silent tomb; and the world has never before seen the day, when any nation could present such an array of talent within her councils. And they, succeeded by the present able statesmen, who have been raised up to fill their places; among whom are Albert G. Brown, Jefferson Davis, and O. R. Singleton, of Mississippi; Mr. Benjamin, of Louisiana, and many others whose talents shine resplendent from every State in the Union, and show forth to all mankind that ours is a land of intellect, virtue, and patriotism, and also the land of religion and civilization.

Who is there that cannot admire such a country? Who cannot admire its institutions? Here is a country with already thirty-four States in the Union, each larger than many of the kingdoms in Europe; territory enough to make twenty more, fourteen of which own African slaves, who add greatly to the strength and support of the whole; transporting annually three and a half millions of cotton bales to other countries, by means of slave labor; a country in which the African is more safe and comfortable, better provided for, more civilized, and more happy, than they are in any other nation; with about thirty millions of inhabitants as free as the air they breathe; with no other restriction than that which is for their own benefit and welfare; with a government framed and managed by themselves; with a revenue, by way of duties, of eighty millions of dollars, and a country whose one year's income of revenue could pay the whole national debt; whose flag floats on every sea on the globe; whose citizens are honored and respected among all nations; whose very name of being an American citizen is a sufficient protection against imposition; whose citizens are protected in the enjoyment of their lives, their liberty, and their property, at home and abroad; where all have the high privilege of hearing the gospel of the Lord Jesus Christ preached, and the privilege of worshiping God according to the dictates of their own conscience, without money and without price; and there is none to make them afraid.

And as remarkable as it may seem to many, there is not an individual in the whole nation who pays even one cent of taxes to support and keep up this great government under which they live, and by which they are thus protected. It is kept up and supported by means of the revenue on imported articles taken in exchange for our exports, which are the proceeds of African slave labor. Three and a half million of cotton bales—the product of slave labor—are annually shipped to other countries and exchanged for other articles which are brought to the United States in return, on which a duty is paid sufficient to defray all of the expenses of the country, without resorting to any direct taxation. The only direct taxes which are paid are paid to keep up the State governments, and the county taxes. There are no direct taxes to keep up the great government of the United States; she supplies herself with her own resources.

CHAPTER VII.

The Probable Result of African Slavery.

When we examine into the situation of Africa, and view its position and the condition of its inhabitants, their peculiar color, hair, formation, intellect, and disposition, we are bound to come to this conclusion, that the kinky-headed African negro is different, in many respects, from the white race, and far inferior, in point of intellect and sound reason, physically. They seem incapable of thriving under a republican form of government, and therefore, as a matter of necessity, these people will always, perhaps, live under a despotism. Africa, with her wide-spread territory, can never, under negro rule, be brought under one great government, so as to be governed by one set of laws, under one government, throughout the whole; for the very reason, that the negro is too contracted in his nature for any such a system of government. We had as well suppose that a herd of wild monkeys would frame a system of laws, by which a whole nation would be regularly governed, as to suppose such a thing from the kinky-headed negro.

The consequence is, then, that Africa, an extensive country, abounding in lakes, fine rivers, seas, and beautiful harbors, is cut up and divided into at least one hundred or more different little petty kingdoms or despotisms, among which are the Dahomies, the Barbaries, the Nuflies, the Benins, the Yaouries, the Anzooans, the Ijibuses, the Eboes, and many others too numerous to be here inserted, in the which the voice of the king is their law, and he rules with an iron sway his humble subjects, as far as his jurisdiction extends; and not unfrequently, when they are visited by a white man, they have a great many of their poor subjects butchered like hogs, in order to show their power and authority. And some of their kings have heralds continually standing beside them, proclaiming aloud, from the rising of the monarch in the morning until he lays down to sleep at night, that this is the greatest king alive!

Thus it is, that intestine wars must, of course, continually rage between these little petty princes, until eventually Great Britain, France, or some other civilized nation, will interfere, and conquer the whole country. Place white men to rule over them, convert their country into plantations, and put them to work as slaves, and make them keep order and be at peace with each other; and all nations, finding that they make good slaves, and are by no means revolutionary in their character, will become slaveholders, and the kinky-headed African will be bought and sold like cattle, in every civilized nation of the earth, as slaves to the descendants of Shem and Japheth.

CHAPTER VIII.

*How to make African Slavery Profitable.—Treatment of Slaves.
—Their Houses.—Their Clothing.—Their Food.*

I come now to consider the important part, of the manner of making slavery profitable to the owners. The African slave is, in many respects, very different from any other species of property to the slave owner. In addition to their being property, they are also human beings; and, as such, are entitled to certain privileges and rights under the laws of the country and humanity, which ought to be taken into consideration. I differ with Doctor Nott, an able physician, who has written a treatise on the physical construction of the African. I believe it is his opinion that the negro has no soul; but I think the Doctor is mistaken. Although their soul may be very small, in comparison to that of the white man, yet I believe they have a soul of some sort. Although I have seen horses and dogs which seemed to possess as much understanding as the common African negro, yet the negro seemed to possess the best talent of construction; and, therefore, I consider them superior to the brute creation. Then it becomes the owner of such people, in the government and management of their slaves, to regard them in the light of human beings as well as property, ever bearing in mind that they are human beings as ourselves, possessed of an immortal soul, which must eventually be saved through the intervention of Jesus Christ, our Lord and Saviour, or lost forever. And though slaves, they have been placed under the care and protection of their masters by the decrees of the Almighty Ruler of the universe, to whom the owner will eventually have to answer for his stewardship over all which is here placed in his charge.

The number of slaves owned in the slaveholding States by each individual slaveholder, varies from one slave up to fifteen hundred. There are not very many who just own one slave; for, in such cases, the slave is certain to become so unhappy and discontented—it makes no difference how well he may be treated—that his master is obliged to sell him, and let him have a master who owns more, where he is certain to be well satisfied, if his new master owns over ten, regardless of ill-treatment, hard work, and bad food. In like manner there are but very few slaveholders among the many in the United States who own as many as fifteen hundred or a thousand, owing to the high prices of such property. For a man to own one hundred, is called quite a rich man,—the price of slaves varying, for full-grown slaves, from eight hundred to fifteen hundred dollars each, for common field hands; and as a man who owns slaves must own other property in proportion, any man who owns one hundred slaves, take them large and small, may be said to be worth one hundred and fifty thousand dollars, or on an average of one thousand and five hundred dollars for every slave he owns. It is very rarely the case that, among the many slaveholders in the United States, one can be found who owns a thousand, although I have heard of three brothers who owned about three thousand each—the three Harstons; one of them lived in the State of Mississippi, and the other two in Virginia. A man who owns from one to two hundred, is termed a very rich slaveholder. But there are a great number who own from ten to thirty; and these are termed slaveholders in good circumstances, and who, by using proper industry and economy, can live as well, and have every luxury of life about them to feast upon, and be far more contented than those who own such very large numbers. But in either case the slaveholder is not to be envied; he has his hands full to attend to his slaves, and if he does his duty, he is himself about the greatest slave among them; for on him devolve the care and protection of all the rest, and he is continually kept busy looking after them, seeing that they are properly fed and clothed, and kept in order, and properly provided with bedding and comfortable houses, and other necessaries needed, and having them properly taken care of when sick, supplied with wholesome food and good nurses.

The system of government of a lot of slaves must differ in some respects, according to the number owned. Where a man only owns few, say from ten to twenty, he can see to them himself, and very readily perceive what is necessary to be done or supplied, or readily correct any evil practice among them, where he can be on his farm himself to attend in person to them. But where he cannot remain on his farm to attend in person, or where he owns a great many slaves, and has to place them on different plantations, which is almost invariably the case with those who own over a hundred, they have to trust the management of them to overseers or agents, and, in many instances, the owner of the slaves does not go among them, or on the plantation, once in six months. A great deal, then, depends on the honesty and fidelity of the agent or overseer. And there are but very few, in proportion to number, of this class of men who can be relied on as being strictly honest, true, and faithful; and whenever a wealthy planter can happen to find such, I would advise him to keep him as long as he can, although he has to pay him high wages for his service; for, of all other occupations among men in the slaveholding States, that of a good overseer among negroes pays best among a large number of hands. For, in many cases, the overseer is an unprincipled wretch, who cares nothing for the interest of his employer, and has no feeling of humanity for the slave, and has not been able to manage his own affairs, with no one to work but himself. He applies for the berth of an overseer to a gentleman, to oversee some fifteen or twenty negroes or more; when placed on a farm to himself to manage alone, he immediately commences all kinds of debauchery among the negro women; he knows nothing about management, throws the place into confusion, neglects his business, and sometimes unites with a company of thieves and steals his employer's negroes and horses, and ships them off by other rogues; and with a farm on the best land in the country, with twenty hands to work with, every convenience at hand, instead of gaining some three or four thousand dollars annually for his employer, at the end of the year he has not cleared expenses by two thousand dollars; and everything on the place is in disorder and confusion; and should his employer happen to discharge him a month or two before his time is out, in order to keep from being ruined, he thinks it is a very hard case to be cut out of a month or two months' wages, although he has, in reality, made nothing for his employer, and run him to great expense.

Therefore, it is highly important for the slaveholder, when he leaves his property in the hands of an overseer, to select some man of known reputation and ability as such, to take charge of it; and even then, the oftener the owner can visit his farm, and see how things are managed, the better it will be for him; for the frequent presence of the owner will show to the overseer that he feels a deep interest in the farm, and the slightest neglect will be discovered; and this will add a spur to his energy, and make him more careful. Good steel will sometimes get dull, and need whetting. And should the slaveholder discover that he has been deceived in his overseer—that he either lacks capacity or principle—he ought, unhesitatingly, to discharge him at once; for, if he keeps him, his overseer will ruin him.

Farming and managing of negroes is a science; to become perfect in it requires practice and experience, and unless an overseer has some practice and experience, he certainly is not qualified to take charge of a farm, with a number of hands to work it: he ought first to serve an apprenticeship under some one who is qualified. Such might make a good driver, or under-overseer, on a farm where the owner was present, or a principal overseer to manage and direct the business; but would never answer as the principal superintendent in the absence of the owner. What lawyer is there who would trust a young stripling to manage a case in court of much importance, in which he was concerned, immediately after he was admitted? or what doctor is there who would trust his life, in a critical case of sickness, to the management of a young physician as soon as he had obtained his license? I can readily answer, none. They will do to ruin novices: so with green overseers. A man who is truly an overseer himself, will never trust his farm in the hands of a green overseer; he will let such go to ruin novices, such as do not know the difference.

But want of principle is even more important than lack of qualification. If your overseer should ever once betray you, or grossly deceive you, trust him no further; he will continually do so as long as you keep him, and the quicker you get rid of him the better. If he is a rascal, it is vain for you to try to make an honest man of him; it will come as natural for him to deceive you, as it is for a wolf to catch a sheep: he will promise to do so no more, and the very first opportunity he has, he will do the same thing over again, according to his nature.

I would not advise the discharging of an overseer for every little vice or error, if he would suit otherwise; for, of course, we must make the necessary allowance for the frailties of human nature, and put up with some faults and failings, where they do not amount to anything very injurious; but in the case of palpable want of qualification, or willful deception, set them adrift without ceremony: it is much better to have no overseer, than to have one who would ruin you, and breed disaffection among your negroes.

It is not harsh treatment, or much whipping among negroes, which causes them to behave themselves, or do the most work; on the contrary, a good overseer is always kind to the slaves, and seldom or never has to whip one. By his good management, every one knows the particular duty which he has to perform, knows what to do in the morning, having his particular work allotted to him the evening before, and everything moves on in order and decorum. I want no better evidence of a bad overseer and a mean manager, than to see him always whipping the negroes. It is the best evidence in the world that he does not know how to manage, and that he is punishing the negroes because they did not know what to do, because he himself did not know what to tell them to do, and he whips the negroes for his own faults; when, if he had given them the proper instructions about their business, as a good overseer would have done, the negroes would have gone to work without any noise or difficulty. It is only the wagon which is out of order, and without grease, that makes the creaking noise; the one which is well oiled, and in fine order, moves gracefully and smoothly along, without noise or disturbance.

Slave property, like everything else, the better it is treated, and the better it is attended to, the better it will prosper, and the more profit it will yield to the owners. Therefore, in addition to the imperative duty of the slaveholder, it is good economy, and more profitable, for him to feed his negroes and clothe them well, according to the season of the year; the clothing should be cotton for the summer, and woolen for the winter; and also to provide them with good, comfortable houses and bed-clothing, and make them take care of what he gives them.

CHAPTER IX.

How to Construct their Houses.

As it is always better for the slaves not to be too much crowded, and in such a state they will be more cleanly and prosperous put off in families than they would to be crowded, the first thing to be done, when a man gets a family of slaves, or where one of his negro women takes a husband, is to prepare a suitable house for them, and place them to themselves as a separate family, and suffer no other negro on the farm to intrude upon them. Let the man consider it as his house and his premises, and say to him, If any other negro comes in your house who you do not want there, order him out, and if he will not go, inform your master of it, or the overseer, and he will make him go. In this way they have a better opportunity of taking care of their goods, and of being more neat and cleanly than they otherwise would be. Besides, the women are not so apt to prove inconstant to their husbands as they otherwise would be, and much fighting and contention among the men are avoided. A negro woman who, otherwise, would be lewd and breed contention, where the family were crowded in a room with others, situated to themselves would be tolerably virtuous, and therefore much disturbance avoided; and they will be much better satisfied, produce more children, and take better care of them. And never more than one family ought to be permitted to occupy the same house.

Then, in order to make the house comfortable, I would advise a cabin to be built about fifteen feet wide, with two rooms; one for their sleeping-room, the other for their cooking-room, and to hold their provisions and loose plunder; with a chimney, made of brick or stone, in the center, with two fire-places, one for each room. The sleeping-room should be about fifteen feet square; the cooking-room fifteen feet one way, and about ten feet the other. This may be effected by making a room twenty-five feet one way, and fifteen the other, and running a partition through the building, cutting off ten feet at one end, which would make the two rooms. The floor should be tongued and grooved, so as to be perfectly air-tight; and there should be one window to each room, about three by four feet; and the walls of the house should be made air-tight, or nearly so. If the house is built of logs, it ought to be chinked and daubed well with clay, so as to keep out the cold winter winds; if a framed building, the weather-boarding will make it tight enough; and it is best to have the door on the south side, so situated that the north winds will not blow in on them when the door is opened. The house should be about nine feet high in the story, and covered over with good boards or shingles, so that it will not leak a drop; and there should be a number of wooden pins placed in the house about in different places in the wall, about as high up as the slaves can conveniently reach, for the purpose of hanging their clothes and other articles on.

It is sometimes the case that the negro will come in from work wet, and sit down by the fire and go to sleep; and if they have an open house in the winter, he wakes up, finds the north wind is pouring in on him, and his fire has gone out, and he has no more wood to make another; hence he sickens with cold or pleurisies, and dies, all for the want of a comfortable house; when, if his house was close and comfortable, if his fire did go out, he would be in a close, comfortable room, where he could sleep all night without freezing or feeling uncomfortably cold. Thus the life of a negro, worth one thousand dollars, may be saved, frequently, to the owner, by building a comfortable cabin, which would not cost fifty dollars.

It is best to build the houses in rows, and have them not very far apart; but, at the same time, put them off a sufficient distance from each other so that, in case one should take fire, it will not burn up any of the rest; say about fifty yards apart. It is best not to have them too far from each other, for the reason that they would be more apt to harbor runaways, unbeknown to each other, and not so easily managed; but just of sufficient, convenient distance from each other to be safe from catching fire from each other. As it is the case sometimes, in spite of all the caution that can be used, fire will break out; and then, if the houses are within catching distance, they may all burn up.

CHAPTER X.

Mode of Clothing the Slaves.

Having treated of the mode of building negro-houses for their comfort and support, I come next in order to treat of the mode of clothing the negro, which is an important item, in order to make the slave profitable and thrifty; and of all other property owned in the United States or elsewhere, good attention to slaves will pay a better profit to the owner than any other species of property; for it is as easy to attend to the comfort of a slave, worth fifteen hundred dollars, as it is to a horse worth fifty dollars, and more so; and if we will only look around us, and survey nature as far as our feeble observation extends, we will find that nothing will prosper without attention, and the better anything is cultivated or attended to, the more it will thrive, the better it will appear, and the more service it will render the owner. Therefore, let an owner of slaves be ever so penurious, or destitute of feelings of humanity, if he is a man of sense, he will treat his slaves kindly, and clothe them well, for his own interest, for it is to his interest decidedly to do so; but apart from all this, every slaveholder has a double obligation resting on him, to induce him to clothe and feed his slaves well: first is the duty he owes to his God, who has placed him in charge of his slaves, to whom he will have eventually to account for his stewardship here, and to himself, to provide for his own welfare, in taking care of his property and rendering it profitable; and the next, is his duty toward the slave as a human being, over whom he has control, and who continually looks to his owner for protection and support.

In the first place, the owner has the complete control of his slave, and of all his earnings; the slave is entirely deprived of any means of furnishing either food or clothing for himself; the owner has all of the profits arising from the slave's labor, let it be much or small, and has the direction of the slave in what he shall do; and of all people on earth, the slave is kept the most regular at work. When his owner says come, he has to come; when he says go, he has to go; and their food and their clothing is all they get for their services; therefore, by every principle of justice, humanity, and religion, it is the duty of the owner of the slave to feed and clothe his slaves well; to give them good, strong clothing, suitable to the season and the work they have to perform, and good, wholesome food.

In the next place, if the owner of slaves should lose a slave for the want of a blanket to keep him warm at night, or for the want of a good, strong suit of woolen clothes in the winter, which would not cost ten dollars, he would, perhaps, suffer a pecuniary loss of a thousand dollars in the death of the slave, because he was too stingy to spend ten dollars for clothes to keep him alive. In this way stingy men keep themselves poor, by their own meanness, through an erroneous idea of true economy, while those who are more liberal grow rich by making the proper appropriation for the comfort and support of their slaves. One loses a thousand dollars' worth of slave-property, trying to cheat his slave out of the value of a suit of clothes not worth ten dollars; and the other man saves a thousand dollars for a suit of clothes to make his slave comfortable. Then, the next question which arises is, how shall we clothe them, how much shall we give them, and at what season of the year, and with what kind of clothing?

Negroes who labor should be furnished with at least three or four strong suits of new clothes each, every year, and two strong, new pair of shoes. They should have at least two summer suits of cotton, and one or two woolen suits for winter; one cotton suit should be given to them the first of April, the next summer suit given to them the first of August; and their winter suits the first of December. They should have a pair of shoes given the first of October, and a pair the first of January; and before they are given to them, have the leather well saturated with a mixture of beeswax, rosin, and tallow, about equal parts of each; this will make the leather last twice as long as it would without it; and if applied to leather of any kind, will add greatly to its durability. The clothes should be given to them at different periods in this way; for, if they were all given to them at once, they being naturally careless, would not take care of them, and would let them lay out and rot; but, by giving them the clothes as they need them, if any are left to be wasted, it will be the old, worn-out suit, and the new ones will be taken care of. They should each be furnished with a trunk or box to keep their clothes in, with a lock and key to lock them up, and a paper of large needles and plenty of thread, and a thimble, in order to be able to mend their clothes when they are torn. They should also, each grown negro, be furnished with a good mattress, made of cotton and shucks, or wool or dried moss; and should always have on hand three good blankets for each grown negro, and two good blankets for each child, in order to keep them comfortable and warm in the winter. A family of a man and his wife and six children ought to have at least three mattresses and eighteen blankets; they may not have to use them all at once regularly, but there are a few excessive cold nights sometimes in the course of the winter, when all would be needed for the comfort of the family. Each family should be furnished with an ax and weeding-hoe, a wash-tub, water-pail, oven-skillet, frying-pan, sifter, and wash-pot, to be kept continually at their houses, for the use of the family, so that they would not have to borrow from each other; and the woman ought to have one-half of every Saturday, to wash their clothes, and be made to wash them. Some men will not furnish their slaves with such comforts, and, therefore, they have a great many to die for the want of them. Suppose, for instance, a slave returns from his work at nine o'clock at night, in the winter, in cotton-picking time, which is frequently the case, and has no ax to chop his wood, and, perhaps, has to bring his wood on his shoulder for a mile or more, as is the case on some of the large plantations, where there are a great number of slaves, and then has to cook his supper and his food for the next day; as he has no ax to chop his wood, or has to borrow one from some of the rest after they have gotten through, how is it possible for that slave to make him a good fire and do his cooking properly? He cannot do it at all; therefore, he gathers such sticks as he can find, makes a poor fire, about half cooks his provisions, and, from fatigue and exhaustion, falls down on the floor and goes to sleep; should the weather be cold and he wet, he has not fire enough to dry himself; he lays down in his wet clothes, the fire goes out, he has no more wood to renew it, takes cold and dies, when his life might have been saved merely by having a few of the comforts of life about him, which would not have cost the owner twenty dollars all together. But negroes will be wasteful, and when these things are furnished, will frequently trade them off to other negroes, or throw them away. This evil must be remedied by inspecting their houses frequently, and seeing that they have them and keep them in order. It is sometimes the case, that negroes will have every comfort they need one winter, and the next winter they will have nothing at all, having permitted their goods to be thrown about and wasted during the summer; and when the ensuing winter comes on, they are entirely destitute, and unless their owners will see to it and furnish them again, they will risk the terrors of the winter in destitution, rather than complain to their owners, for fear of being whipped for their carelessness. Thus it is, that not unfrequently a woman who has four or five likely children, throws her bed-clothes away in the summer, lets them lay out and rot, and when the winter comes on, the owner, not having inquired into the matter, believing she has taken the proper care of her bedding, supposes she is well furnished, when one by one the children take cold, catch the croup, and die; while the owner spends five times as much in doctor's bills for them during the time than would purchase them a new supply, and loses his negroes besides. Therefore, on the first day of October, in every year, and January and July, at three times during the year, the owner should go to every negro-house and inspect everything they have, and enter it in a book, and see what each one needs; and if they should waste their goods, or throw them away, give them a flogging for their carelessness, and be sure and furnish them with more. Some men will get angry with their slaves if they waste their goods, and will not furnish them any more in consequence of it; and will say to them, As you have wasted your clothes, or thrown away your blankets, or your ax, you may now go without; I will buy you no more to throw away. This is very bad economy, and such a course frequently costs the owner the value of the slave by his death, for the want of them. The course to be pursued is for the owner to give them a light whipping for their negligence, and charge them particularly to be more careful in the future, and then give them another supply immediately. In this way, the owners will attach their slaves to them, will make them healthy, cheerful, and prosperous, and add greatly to the wealth and interest of the slaveholder.

Again, it frequently happens that slaves return from their work at night wet, and it is raining, when it is very difficult, if they have the means, for them to procure wood to make their fires; and if they have to hunt about in the dark for it, they are almost sure to go without, or be so very badly supplied that they materially suffer for want of it.

Therefore, to remedy this evil, the slaves should be particularly charged and required to keep continually on hand, under their houses, or under their beds in some dry place, wood enough to make at least two good fires; and when an occasion of that kind arrived, they could use their dry wood, and be enabled to have good fires, without going out in the rain after dark to hunt it; and then the next day they could replace it. This is very important to be observed, and the owner or overseer ought to see to it continually, and make them keep a supply on hand for bad weather.

Again, there are generally two or three spells of excessive cold weather during the winter season in the South, which lasts for a week or ten days at a time, when the ground becomes frozen. At such times as this, slaves ought not to be forced out to work before sunrise in the morning; and then they ought to be permitted to return to their houses by, or before the sun goes down, so as to have ample time to provide a plenty of wood and fix comfortable before it is dark; and the women, during such cold days, ought to remain at the house with their children, in order to take care of them even if they do nothing except to take care of their children during such cold spells, as they will be worth more at such times in taking care of their children than their work would possibly be in the field; and their children ought all to be furnished with good, woolen clothes in the winter, to protect them from the cold, and prevent them from catching on fire, for in the winter time children will hover near the fire, and if they are clothed in cotton, they are apt to take fire, when wool will not burn; and besides, it is much more comfortable and will last longer than cotton, and costs but very little more. Slaveholders who will pursue this course, will find that they will be richly rewarded in the health and increase of their slaves; and that the little additional expense they are at in procuring and preparing comforts for their slaves is money well invested, and will pay better than the same amount invested in anything else.

In the course of the last twenty-five years I have had the management of from ten to one hundred slaves at a time, and during the whole time have only lost one slave who was large enough to work, and she was an old woman who died with old age, whose descendants numbered over a hundred at the time of her death, and only four slave children during the whole twenty-five years. The consequence has been, that the increase of my slaves have added much more to the value of my property than the amount of their labor.

I had a neighbor, a few years ago, who owned fifty slaves. He was one of the most prudent, economical men I ever was acquainted with: he lived almost entirely within himself. With but very little expense he made his own cooper's ware, done his own blacksmith's work, tanned his leather and made his own shoes, clothed his family, white and black, with cloth of his own manufacture, and was at no expense, except the purchase of his iron, sugar, and coffee. The consequence was, that he was enabled to save more money than ordinary men, which he invested entirely in the purchase of slaves; but at the same time he devoted a great deal of attention to his slaves, and saw that they were properly cared for and fed, and well clothed, with good, comfortable dwellings. The consequence was, that in the course of sixteen years he had purchased fifty slaves with the money he had saved, and had raised one hundred and fifty, having raised just three times as many as he had purchased, and those which he had raised were the most valuable; and all the while made larger crops to his force than any other planter in the neighborhood, all by treating his slaves well and having them properly attended to; and I do not suppose that, during the whole time, a single slave under his charge was ever so badly whipped as to make a scar.

CHAPTER XI.

Mode of Feeding Slaves.

We will next in order consider the proper mode of feeding slaves, in order to make them profitable, which, like clothing, is a very important item in the management of slaves—one of far more importance than many persons are aware of who are not physiologists. A certain quantity of nutriment is essentially important, both for the vegetable and animal kingdom; and when deprived of the necessary quantity or quality, either the animal or vegetable will wither, dwindle away, and become feeble and weak, and, of course, less fit for use. Although it may receive enough to sustain life, it is more susceptible to destruction, and less able to withstand hardships and of performing the service for which it was designed, than it would be when amply supplied; for instance, a horse may be fattened on green food, but when put to service, he will soon tire and give way; while one that is fattened on good dry food will do double the quantity of service of the other which is fattened on the green food, and will not tire or give out. Any person who has been used to the management of horses knows this to be true by observation, and it is more or less so with all animals; their flesh will partake, more or less, of the nature, in point of durability, of the food which they eat, and when put to hard labor their appetite will crave that kind and quantity of food best calculated to enable them to proceed in their labor. You may take an able-bodied man and put him behind the counter to sell goods, where the labor is light and no excessive exertion is required, and his stomach would reject fat bacon or pork; he would not, perhaps, eat more than a pound of meat in a week, and his appetite would be satisfied with light food and weak diet, and he would be able to progress with his business. But take the same man and put him to malling rails, rolling of logs, chopping down trees, and doing such heavy, rough work, and he would eat a pound of fat bacon every day, and other strong food with it, and relish it more than he would any dainty, because it is absolutely necessary for him, in order to strengthen him and enable him to perform his work. The consequence is, that slaves which are well fed with good wholesome food will do double the work with more ease than they would do scantily fed; and it is, therefore, good economy and a money-saving business to feed your slaves well, and give them plenty to eat, if meat has to be purchased even at high prices for the purpose.

As to the mode of giving slaves their food, there are many methods used. Some give it to them every week, once a week, a week's allowance at a time, and let them cook it themselves. Some give it to them twice a week in the same way; and others have it cooked for them. I think, however, the best plan is to have some of it cooked for them, and let them also cook a little for themselves; for when slaves have to work all day in the summer season, and return home at dark when the nights are short, and have to make their own fires and do their own cooking, they frequently eat it raw, or go without. It is, therefore, best to have their cooking done for them on large farms. Let every negro have a bucket large enough to hold his day's provision, with his number on it, which number should be plainly and distinctly marked; have the provision cooked neat and clean, and each negro's day's allowance put in the buckets, so that when they return at night they have nothing to do but call at the cookhouse and receive their cooked provisions in their buckets, and eat their supper and go to bed, so that they can have a good night's rest and be ready for work in the morning. On Saturday nights, provisions should be furnished them to do them for two days, until Monday night, and let them cook it themselves as they may choose.

The quantity of bacon necessary for a common field-hand is about four and a half pounds a week, with vegetables and a quart of meal per day, or a pound of flour per day. As bread, every farmer ought to raise as many sweet potatoes as his family could consume; they are an excellent food for slaves, and when fed with abundantly, will save other provisions, and negroes are very fond of them.

They are easily raised, and to the quantity necessary for a man's family, they pay better than any other crop. Corn-field peas also are a fine vegetable for negroes,—turnips, collards, and Irish potatoes. Every farmer ought to raise abundance of such vegetables for the use of his slaves; for if he has a plenty of potatoes and peas or beans for his negroes, they will not require so much meat, and the slaves are very fond of such diet, and such vegetables are very easily raised on any kind of soil in the slaveholding region. Irish potatoes and pumpkins are also valuable as a vegetable for slaves, and may be raised in great abundance, with but little expense.

The women who have children should each of them have an extra bucket, in which a sufficient quantity of food should be placed for their children at night and morning, and during the day there should be a trusty old woman to take care of them and feed them; but it will not do to trust any negro to take care of another's children entirely, for they, in such cases, are sure to neglect them, and let them die for want of attention, or suffer greatly; for they generally will not take good care of their own children unless their owners see to it, and make them do it, and they are certain not to take as good care of each other's as they would of their own. Therefore, slaveholders ought never to separate small children from their mothers, and place them entirely in the care of others for weeks at a time; if they do, the loss of a majority of their little negroes will be the fatal consequence.

CHAPTER XII.

Women and Children—How to Treat Them.

It is the custom on some of the large plantations on the Mississippi River and elsewhere for the owner of slaves during the sickly season to take the children to some place on the high lands for the purpose of their being more healthy, and placing them under the care of some old negress to feed, manage, and take care of during the summer, supposing that in this way the children would be less apt to die, and would be better taken care of. But this is altogether a mistake; for wherever the experiment has been tried, it has proved fatal in ninety-nine cases out of a hundred. The little negroes have frequently, in such cases, died for the want of the proper attention, when it was supposed by the owner they died from common sickness.

Notwithstanding the negro race is far inferior, in point of natural affection, to the whites, they, nevertheless, possess a strong attachment for their own children, and are endued with that parental care for their own brood which is common to all animals, without which the world would soon be depopulated—an instinct which has been so wisely bestowed upon all living animals by the great Creator and Preserver of the universe, in order that they should take care of their young, and provide for them until they were enabled to shift for themselves. And although they would neglect the child of one of their best friends, and suffer it to die with starvation when under their immediate care for the want of a little attention, being prompted by the impulses of natural affection, they would place themselves to a great deal of trouble to attend to their own children and administer to their wants. Therefore, I would say to those persons who own women and children, not to separate them when the child is under ten years old, under any pretense whatever; if the mother has to stay in the swamp and work, let the children stay with her. Give them a plenty to eat, and they will be far better attended to by their mother, and less liable to die, than when under the care of any other, although the climate may be unhealthy. It is not half so unhealthy as the care of a stranger who cares nothing for them; and they will be sure to fare better when their mother can see them once every day. And if the woman has a husband on the plantation, let them all stay on the same farm together: he can greatly aid in attending to the children at night.

I knew a gentleman who owned two plantations: one was on the Mississippi River, near Natchez; the other out in the hills, about fifteen miles from the river; and, in order that his young negroes should be more healthy, he took them from the river farm, and placed them under the care of a trusty old negress, out at his plantation on the high lands. The consequence was, that a great many of the children died; the old woman attributed it to nothing more than common sickness, which human nature is subject to, and averred, in the most positive terms, that she had attended strictly to them. The gentleman pursued this plan for two summers, and the fatality was the same among his young negroes in both summers. At length he concluded that it certainly could be no worse on the river, and he would let their mothers have charge of them in the swamp. The consequence was, that his little negroes became more healthy, and he very seldom ever lost one. He was then convinced that it was bad policy to separate negro children from their mothers, in order to have them taken care of.

The experiments have been tried by many others, and the result was invariably the same, as far as my knowledge extends. I would, therefore, recommend to all slaveholders to keep their negro children with their mothers, and not to permit them to be separated; to attend to them in person, and see that everything was furnished necessary for their comfort and support, and to give the women who have children time to nurse and to attend to them. And those who have negroes in their charge to hire out for the benefit of orphan children, would always do better to hire families in one lot together—a man, his wife, and all the children under ten years of age—so, if one should get sick, the others who are nearly related will attend to them. I have known a great many negroes hired out to the highest bidder, and those that were hired in families always done better and prospered more than those who were hired from their families. I have known several instances of children being hired from their mothers, where the child contracted cold, for the want of their mothers to attend to them, in very cold weather, and died. Children will not take the necessary care of their bedding and clothes, so as to have them in order for use in cold weather, and it is useless to expect it; and, when hired out by themselves, will frequently lay down and go to sleep without any bedding at all in very cold weather, and therefore freeze, for the want of a friend to hunt up their blanket, and throw it over them.

One of the greatest pieces of economy of the slaveholder is, to see that his negro women and children are properly attended to. They are more hardy, generally, than the whites, and, when properly attended to, will increase much faster; and the same care and attention devoted to the comfort of the women and children among negroes, will enrich the owner faster in that way than any other.

The owner of slaves should never permit his women, while pregnant, to be flogged; there would be danger from the excitement occasioned by the whipping, not only of destroying the child, but the mother also. Women are much more apt to die from a miscarriage than a natural birth; and a very slight whipping in such cases might produce a miscarriage, and cause death in both the mother and child.

And again, there are a few cruel men, who are in the habit of using a paddle on their women, or permitting it to be done by their overseers. This practice is not only indecent in the highest degree, and to be condemned as brutal and inhuman, but it is ruinous and destructive to the women; it is almost sure to produce a miscarriage, if the woman is in a pregnant state, and not unfrequently causes the womb of the woman to fall and destroy her general health as long as she lives; and I would say to all slaveholders, strictly to enjoin it on your overseers not to use a paddle on any of the women under any pretext whatever, and never to whip them on the bare backs, so as to cut the skin; they can be just as easily managed to whip them over the shoulders, with their clothes on, as to whip them on the naked back. They should never be cruelly whipped or abused; thirty-nine lashes with a small switch is enough to give them for any moderate offense, and will frequently answer a better purpose than a more severe whipping. There are other modes of punishment which frequently answer a much better purpose than whipping, and are much less liable to injure the slave; for instance, to lock them up in the jail for a day or two in solitary confinement. This will frequently do more good than whipping; and every large farmer ought to have a jail of some sort on his plantation; it is much better than a cowhide to prevent slaves from running about after dark.

The main object in all punishment is to cow the spirit and produce a reformation in the offender, and that mode is always the best which will produce the desired effect with the least physical injury; and when the slave is cowed, every lick he gets afterwards only tends to lessen his value, and makes him less able to render service to his owner. If one lick will cow the slave, stop right there, he needs no more; the person who whips, if he is any judge at all of the disposition of negroes, can tell in a moment when the negro is cowed—he will begin to beg and plead for mercy; until he is cowed, he will remain stubborn and sullen. Negroes ought not to be beaten with sticks or large hickories; such only deaden the flesh and disable the negro; a small, keen switch or whip will hurt worse for the moment and do less injury, and produce the desired effect much quicker, than a large one.

Again, negro women ought not to be forced to work out in rainy, wet weather, for this reason at least, once each month they have their monthly courses on them, and if they should get their feet wet at such times, it causes a sudden stoppage of the menstrual discharges, and produces severe sickness, attended frequently with violent pain in the head and parts of the body; and it is frequently the case, that the general health of the woman is destroyed through life, by being exposed to bad, wet weather at such times; and it is much better for the owner to lose a few days of the labor of their women at such times during the year, than to have the risk of destroying the general health of the slave during life by exposure.

CHAPTER XIII.

The Mode of arranging Out-houses on a Plantation—Jail, Ballroom, Church, Hospitals, with the Mode of Treating the Sick, and evil Consequence of the Use of Spirituous Liquors.

As to the quantity of out-houses on each plantation, much will depend on the size of the family and quantity of negroes on the farm; but, in all cases, every farm ought to have a sufficient quantity of out-buildings to answer every purpose with convenience, so as not to be too much crowded, in order that everything may have its proper place, so as to be arranged in order; for the better everything is arranged, and the most perfect order kept, the greater quantity of labor can be performed with the least trouble and expense. Thus:—

> Order is slavery's first law—and this confessed,
> Some are and must be greater than the rest.

So, there should be a house for every purpose needed on every farm.

And on every plantation where there are as many as forty slaves, there ought to be a plantation-jail of some sort for the purpose of locking up and keeping confined such slaves as cannot be kept from running about in the neighborhood after night, and for the purpose of confining unruly negroes for awhile, instead of corporal punishment. It will sometimes have a better effect to lock a negro up in jail and keep him confined all day on Sunday, than to give him a hundred stripes; and inasmuch as the very object of punishing slaves is to make them behave themselves, that kind of punishment which will effect a reformation with the least injury to the slave, is the most preferable.

I once owned a negro woman, who was in the habit of being insolent and impudent to her mistress. I tried flogging, but it done but little good; at length, I confined her a day or two in prison, without any other punishment, and it had the desired effect; she dreaded the prison worse than the lash.

Again, when negroes are in the habit of strolling about in the neighborhood after night, they may be whipped for it, and still

15

they will continue their practice; they will wait until their owners or overseers go to bed, and will then start out visiting, sometimes after midnight, and walk five or six miles to see their neighbors, and return home again before daybreak in the morning; the consequence is, that the slave is wholly unqualified for service that day, and is frequently made sick by such exposure and loss of sleep; and sometimes has a protracted spell of sickness in consequence of such exposure, all of which may be remedied by confining him a few nights in prison; put him in after supper, and let him out at daylight in the morning, until he reforms. If there is a negro on the place guilty of running about after dark in the neighborhood, without his owner's or overseer's consent, he can be very easily found out, and by punishing him a few nights in prison, he will soon quit it and behave himself; and the very presence of the jail will sometimes have its effect without using it, for negroes would much prefer to be flogged to solitary confinement.

Again, women, when in a state of pregnancy, ought never to be whipped, for causes before mentioned. Flogging at such times might destroy both mother and child; and when they require correction for misconduct, it is far better to lock them up in jail for a few hours than to whip them; but always be certain, if the weather is cold, to see that they have a plenty of blankets to keep them warm on such occasions, otherwise they might freeze or contract severe cold. It will not cost much to erect a private jail on a farm, as almost any kind of a building will answer for the purpose, as those on the outside will never try to break him out; a little log building, ten feet square, will be sufficient, with a common stock lock; two hands can build one in three days complete.

And there should also be a house constructed for a ball-room, on every farm where there are as many as forty slaves, for the amusement of those who wish to dance; that they may have an opportunity of indulging in this kind of pleasure at home, instead of having to seek for it elsewhere. All nations of people, both civilized and savage, appear to be fond of dancing; and the nearer they approach to a savage state, the more they are delighted with such exercises; and until I am convinced to the contrary, I shall be of the opinion that it is an advantage, both to the slaves and the slaveholder, for them to be permitted occasionally to have a ball or dance on the plantation with such as prefer it.

The mind of man is so constructed that it must be employed at something: it will not remain idle; and when not engaged in something innocent, it will invariably be engaged in something vile and mischievous; hence the Roman emperors encouraged public plays and exhibitions for the amusement of the populace, and the Olympic games were instituted and kept up at great expense and trouble for the amusement of the people; and many wise rulers have encouraged sports and amusements among their people for the purpose of amusing their minds. and giving them something new to feast upon. All men are fond of a change occasionally; and after being confined to close business for several months together, the mind naturally seeks for something to amuse it, and if these amusements cannot be had near home, it will seek them abroad. And if the slaves on a farm can have a little dance on the Fourth of July and on Christmas, with something a little extra to eat at such times, they will think and talk about it for months before it takes place, and will have their minds on the frolic which they expect to have, with many pleasing anticipations, instead of insurrection and vile mischief; and after the frolic is over, they will have something to talk and laugh about—some of their awkwardness in the frolic—for months.

The owner or overseer ought in such case to be always present, in order to prevent disturbances, and ought never to permit spirituous liquors to be used on such occasions, under any pretext whatever, and on no other occasion among negroes, for they are the worst kind of savages when drunk, and it is very seldom the case, when negroes get spirituous liquors, in a crowd or assemblage, but that some of them are killed. Owners of slaves should always see to that, and never permit their slaves to indulge in the use of intoxicating spirits. I have known very serious injuries committed by negroes when they were intoxicated, and therefore they ought never to be permitted to use intoxicating liquors as a beverage; it produces temporary mental derangement with all classes, white men as well as negroes, and it is to be deplored that any rational being should use it as a beverage; it blights a man's prospects, destroys his constitution, depraves his appetite, distresses his friends, impoverishes his family, degrades his character, sinks him in his own estimation and that of others, casts a vail over his merit, if he has any, and is the forerunner of vice, and mother of wretchedness and degradation in all its forms. I have been a practicing lawyer for over twenty-five years, and of the great multitude of cases which I have witnessed the trial of for crimes, in the courts of the country. it is strange to tell, that nineteen out of twenty of the crimes committed had their origin, either directly or indirectly, from the use of intoxicating, spirituous liquors, and could be traced to that source.

Next in order, on every large farm there ought to be a church, or place of worship, where the owner or overseer could occasionally assemble the slaves for the purpose of hearing the gospel of Jesus Christ preached to them. This is an imperative duty on the slaveholder, where his farm is so situated that his slaves cannot conveniently leave home to attend church, for him to employ some preacher to visit his farm occasionally, and preach to his slaves, that they may have the benefit of hearing the gospel preached. Those who embrace religion will always make good, obedient servants, as it is one of the injunctions of the Holy Bible, that servants should be obedient to their masters; and unless the owner of slaves on large plantations should employ a preacher to visit his farm and preach to his slaves, many of them may live to a good old age, and die without knowing anything about the gospel of Jesus Christ here in this enlightened Christian land of ours. If a preacher could be employed to preach to them once a month, or once in two months, it might be sufficient. It would hardly be supposed, that any slaveholder would refuse to let his slaves go to church in the neighborhood on Sunday, if there was preaching handy or near at hand; but in many cases farms are so inconveniently situated that there is no church near enough for the masses of the slaves to attend; in such case it is nothing more than justice to the slave for the owner to procure a preacher to visit the farm occasionally—but always have a white man to preach to them. Experience has taught us, that it will not do to suffer negroes to preach. In the first place, their want of Bible knowledge disqualifies them; in the second, they are ignorant and superstitious, and are very apt to preach some of their own superstitious notions as the true doctrine of the Bible, and produce wrong impressions; and in the next place, they are easily flattered, and very soon begin to feel very consequential; and as soon as they begin to be regarded with a degree of reverential awe, as they soon would be by the ignorant negroes, they would begin to regard themselves as possessing very great inspiration, and not unfrequently stir up the negroes, over whom they can exercise an influence, to disaffection and insurrection.

Preaching, properly administered, is attended with much good, both to the slave and master; but, when improperly used, may result in great injury. We may as well say that a man ought not take medicine from a skillful physician, when he is dangerously sick, because there are quacks who know nothing about medicine practicing the profession, who do their patients an injury and sometimes kill them, as to say a slaveholder ought not to have his slaves preached to by a pious, good, white preacher, because an ignorant negro preacher would do them an injury. Negroes are possessed of an immortal soul, and, therefore, their owners should see that they are not deprived of the benefit of the gospel of Christ, the Lord and Saviour of us all.

THE HOSPITAL.

Next in order of buildings on the farm is the hospital. On every farm, where there are as many as twenty slaves, there should be a building erected, according to the number in the family, of sufficient dimensions, and with a sufficient number of rooms, as a hospital, where the sick can be properly nursed and attended to by good, careful nurses, and supplied with such comforts as they need during their sickness; and, therefore, a building of this description is one of the most valuable and important on every plantation, and no large slaveholder should ever be without one. Those who never have had one—and there are many such—if they should ever try it, will never after be without one, and will be surprised that they had ever done without it. By the use of the hospital, negroes can be much easier and better attended to when sick, at a much less expense. The sick will there recover much more readily, and be less apt to die, or to impart their sickness to others, or suffer inconvenience by being with others not their nurses, or cause others to suffer inconvenience from them: and while they will be less apt to die in the hospital than in their houses, their recovery will be much more speedy and certain.

This building should be built with a great deal of care, and particular attention should be paid to its construction, so as to have it to contain a sufficient quantity of rooms, so that each sick negro, if possible, might have a comfortable room to himself; and the rooms should be so constructed as to be made very comfortable, either in the winter or summer, with a brick chimney to each room, for fire in the winter, and good, airy, glass windows for a free admission of the air in the summer. It ought to be situated on the plantation not far from the negro houses, in some cool, shady place, where there are a plenty of good, green shade-trees in the summer, that the house may be made as cool and pleasant as possible in the summer. And there should be a separate room to the building as a cook-room, so that when their provisions were being prepared, the room might not be made uncomfortable by the fire or scent of the provisions. Each room for the sick should be supplied with a good mattress and bedstead, with other necessary bedding to suit the season, a water-bucket, and every other necessary convenience for sick persons, and all should be kept in neat and clean order. And when any of the slaves are sick, have them taken to the hospital, and supplied with a good nurse; and increase the number of nurses as the number of sick increases, so that every sick negro shall be well and properly attended to by their nurses. Their relations should be permitted to visit them at night, and to assist the nurses, if they choose; for sometimes the nurse will neglect the patient, and if their relations come in to see them, the sick negro will complain of the neglect; and the owner can see that they have the proper attention. Each hospital ought to have attached to it at least one good bathing-tub, in which the sick could be bathed all over, as it is highly important, in many cases of sickness, to bathe the patient; and a single bath may sometimes save the life of the slave, when properly administered. Good nursing frequently adds more to the recovery of the patient than medicine; and in every instance good nursing aids the medicine very materially in the cure of the patient.

When a sick negro is taken to the hospital, suppose he has the fever in the summer season, he is placed in a good, comfortable room, in a cool, shady place, has his nurse to wait upon him; he takes medicine, perhaps is kept confined to his bed for a week, during which time he needs particular attention night and day, in order that he may recover; he is, perhaps, up three or four times during the night, from the operation of the medicine; he interrupts no person at all but his nurse, who is placed there for the purpose, and has nothing else to do; after awhile, the sick negro gets easy, drops into a sweet sleep, there is no person stirring or rattling about to interfere with him, he gets through with his sleep, feels refreshed, and his recovery is rapid; he soon gets well and is able to resume his labors again, for the benefit of his owner.

Suppose, again, that there is no hospital or sick-house on the farm, as is the case in thousands of instances where there ought to be one; the negro comes in, in the heat of summer, with the fever on him, his owner or overseer gives him a dose of medicine, and he retires to his cabin. Night comes on, some two or three other slaves of his family come in from work; they have to kindle up a fire to get their suppers, the room becomes heated, the negro with the fever is already nearly dead with a hot fever, and instead of being in a cool, comfortable place where he will not be interrupted, he has to bear the additional scorch of the heating of the room by fire for several hours at a time, until the rest are done cooking their supper, and then bear the warmth that the fire produces afterwards, until it goes out, and not unfrequently dies by this additional aggravation of the disease, when otherwise he would recover without even the aid of medicine. After supper is over, the well negroes, who are now very much fatigued by their day's labor and the fatigue of standing over a hot fire, cooking, lay down, exhausted, to sleep; they rest awhile and are soon aroused from their slumbers by the groans of the sick; his medicine makes him sick and commences its operation; he groans and gets up to attend to the operation of his medicine; the negroes in the room are awakened from their sleep to attend to him; he lays down again, and in the course of an hour or two he rises and interrupts the well negroes again and again in the same way until daylight in the morning, when those who are well, now only half rested by the disturbance of the sick negro, have to repair to the field to resume their daily labor, wearied out from fatigue and the want of rest. During the day some of them are attacked by the fever in the same way; they return to the house, are given a dose of medicine in the same way, sent to their cabin, and then there are two sick ones to annoy the balance of the inmates instead of one, and to be annoyed in the same way; and all this time it does not occur to the owner or overseer the true cause which produces it.

The negroes frequently die in this way, by improper treatment for the want of a sick-house, and their death is attributed, as a matter of course, to the common fatality of the sickness. Whole families are thus frequently made sick and are down at once by this kind of treatment and exposure, when if there had been a sick-house on the place, and the first one who was taken had been sent to it, there would have been no more sickness in that family during the summer; because, when the sick one was properly taken care of at the sick-house, the balance of the family, after getting their supper at night, could lay down and rest easy until daylight, get up, feel refreshed, and cheerfully commence their work in the morning.

Slaveholders frequently lose a great many slaves either for the want of attention or the necessary conveniences; and where the slave is properly attended, and furnished with the necessary conveniences when sick, it is very rarely the case that one ever dies, except from old age. And when they begin to recover from their sickness, they ought to be furnished with good, wholesome food, suitable for persons in such a condition, as at such times the stomach is weak and cannot bear such strong food as when in good health; and the slave ought not to be forced to go out to work too soon after a recovery, or be made to fatigue himself very much shortly after, for fear of a relapse; it is generally the best plan to let the slave remain at his house, after recovering from a severe spell of sickness, until he gets ready to go out to work of his own accord.

CHAPTER XIV.

How to Treat the Women.

On all large farms there are frequently a large portion of the slaves women, and some one or more of them in a state of pregnancy all the while, and this class of slaves, if properly taken care of, are the most profitable to their owners of any others, and if not properly taken care of, are altogether valueless. It is remarkable the number of slaves which may be raised from one woman in the course of forty or fifty years with the proper kind of attention. I have frequently seen the mother, who was a pert, active, old woman under seventy years of age, who could boast of having over a hundred of her posterity living.

But, when they are not properly taken care

of, the children die for the want of attention, and the mother, by being frequently laid up in child-bearing, is valueless as to her labor on the farm. Negro women, when pregnant, ought never to be required to do any very hard, rough work, which would fatigue them, or to lift any heavy weight; neither should they be whipped or abused in any way, but should be treated with sympathy and kindness; and they should be permitted to remain with their children as much as possible, and to remain in the house, without going out to work for their owner, at least five or six weeks after the birth of their child; and when they have to work in the field, let them come to their child three or four times during the day to attend to it, otherwise the infant might die for the want of attention; and very young children require a great deal of nursing, which should never be refused them. Where the owner of the slave appears to exercise a degree of care and attention for the negro children it will act as a stimulant to the mother, and cause her to attend better to her children; but where the owner does not seem to care anything about them, and will not give the mother time to attend to her children, she becomes cowed and disheartened, and will not pay the attention to them that she can, and will frequently be glad to see them die and out of the way.

CHAPTER XV.

A Hint to Overseers.

It is almost invariably the case on plantations where there are over a dozen slaves, the owner has to employ some white man as an overseer to stay on the plantation with the slaves, and direct them in their labor. And it is often the case on large farms, when the owner does not reside on his farm, the overseer has the full charge and control of the negroes and farm, and manages everything according to his own will and pleasure. Therefore, it is very important that an overseer should be a man under a good character, a thorough-going, industrious, business man, one possessing a high sense of honor and honesty as well as anything else; otherwise, instead of being a benefit to his employer, he is a serious injury. Overseeing negroes is like everything else; in order for a man to understand the business well, he must have experience and practice, otherwise he is wholly unfit to take the reins as a principal overseer on a farm; and in order for a man to understand the business, he ought to serve at least five years as a driver or under-overseer, that he may be enabled, when he comes to manage as the principal overseer, to discharge his duty with honor to himself and profit to his employer, and by his management acquire a reputation.

There are great differences in overseers as well as anything else, and of all occupations in the world, a good overseer will pay the employer more than anything else; and the farmer who works twenty hands, who has a first-rate overseer, and pays him a thousand dollars per annum, gets his overseer cheaper than his neighbor who has the same number of hands and a mean overseer which cost him only fifty dollars a year; the good overseer, by his management, will make the farm which he is on clear all expenses, pay his wages, and net the owner from two to three thousand dollars besides; while the mean overseer, by his bad management, will not pay expenses, and frequently, instead of the owner of the farm making a neat profit, he falls behind, and his farm does not clear the expenses by two or three thousand dollars. And where farmers continue to employ such, they will soon get broke by their mean overseers; and the mean overseer will apparently work the negroes harder than the good one, and he is certain to whip a great deal more, for, having no management himself, he suffers everything to get in confusion, and then whips the negroes for what he himself is guilty of.

A great many farmers are ruined by mean overseers; the overseer in such cases ruins himself as well as his employer, for when he is found out to be a mean overseer, no other person wants him, and he is frequently thrown out of employment. It is often the case that a man is not able to manage his own little affairs, with none to work but himself, and being too lazy to work, and unqualified for anything else, he starts out to hunt an overseer's berth, and considers himself worthy of taking charge of a gentleman's farm with fifty or one hundred hands. Such men sometimes succeed in getting employment, and are immediately lifted up in their own estimation, and will splutter about prodigiously for awhile, but as soon as they are left to themselves, will commence neglecting their business; they care nothing about the interests of their employer, so that their wages are going on; they suffer the stock to scatter, the mules and horses to get poor, the whole farm to get out of order, and do not even dream that any person is noticing their management and conduct, while the whole neighborhood, white and black, are noticing every movement and talking about it. Eventually, the owner of the farm comes along; his neighbors tell him how badly his overseer is getting on, he goes to his farm and finds his overseer is worthless, and will ruin him if he keeps him, and he immediately discharges him, and he now has no further prospects as an overseer; he goes around and tries to get in at some other place; he finds that where he is known that no person wants him at any price, and, to his utter surprise, he now finds that instead of not being noticed in his neglect and bad conduct, that every man, woman, and child has been observing his movements in the neighborhood the whole while.

A young man, in such cases, should always remember that when he undertakes to transact business for another, that he has a great deal of character at stake, and that if he is faithful and true, every person around sees it, and will give him credit for his fidelity, but if he is treacherous and trifling, it will also be noticed to his discredit; that when he is at work for his employer, he is at work for himself as much as for his employer, and where he does his best and proves faithful, a great many failings will be looked over for the want of proper information, and that he will improve by the proper kind of exertions and win upon the confidence of his employer, and instead of being discharged, he will be encouraged and his wages will be increased, and he will eventually improve and grow in the confidence of his employer and others who know him, until he will rank as a No. 1 overseer, and can get wages anywhere, and be eagerly sought after; besides, he will have the consciousness of knowing that he has done his duty and proved a blessing to his employers.

It is the duty of the overseer to be continually on the farm, seeing to the interest of his employer; to see to the hogs, the cattle, the horses, the negroes, and everything which requires his attention; to see that the horses and mules are properly fed and watered, that their gear does not gall them; to see that they are kept fat and sleek, for it is a bad sign to see poor horses and mules on a farm where there is a plenty to feed with; it shows too much neglect, or a great want of management. It is also a very bad sign to see the fences down and the gates off of the hinges, and the houses out of repair on a farm. I want no better evidence of bad management than this. I can tell whether a man has a good overseer or not, merely by riding by his farm and looking at his houses and fences; a neat manager will keep all in order without much noise or whipping. The negroes should always know at night what they are required to do in the morning, and the overseer should instruct them how to do their work, and have a particular place to keep everything; every plowman should have his particular horse or mule to manage, and a particular stall for them to stand in, and a particular place to keep their bridles and curry-combs, so that they could get up at any time of a dark night and find them all without a light. In this way, everything will move on in order and regularity; and the overseer should be very cautious, if he went to whip a negro for a slight offense, and the negro should run from him, not to shoot him, but wait until he can hem him and catch him, which would not take very long. A great many negroes will run from the master or overseer when they go to whip them, and it is very wrong to shoot them merely for running from you; it will generally not take very long to catch them afterwards, when they can be sufficiently punished without endangering their lives; and also be cautious and never inflict any cruel or unusual ill-treatment on any slave under your charge, for no humane owner of slaves will like to have his slaves ill-treated in any way, but will think the more of his overseer if he can manage the slaves without punishment.

CHAPTER XVI.

Duties of Masters and Slaveholders.

Every slaveholder should reflect and consider their slaves not only as property, but also as human beings like themselves; that notwithstanding they differ in color and in strength of mind, and condition in life, that the slave is entitled to certain rights which it would be both cruel and unjust to deprive him of: the right of his life, his limbs, of rest on the Sabbath day, and the care and protection of his master, with the privilege of worshiping God in that manner most agreeable to his feelings and the dictates of his conscience. These are privileges which do not interfere at all with the rights of the owner, but only tend to strengthen them, and to better qualify the slaves to render service to their owners. And as the slave receives nothing in return for his labor except victuals and clothes, the owners should always see that their slaves are well fed and clothed. In this way, the slave will be sure to be more cheerful, healthy, and thrifty, and far better qualified to render himself useful and profitable to his owner. Some slaveholders, from a mistaken idea of economy, do not furnish the necessary quantity of food or clothing to their slaves, and seek to grow rich by stinting their slaves in this way; but such a course is the most extravagant after all, and is always attended with ruinous consequences. A slave may sometimes die for the want of a good suit of warm clothes and a good blanket in the winter, which would not cost the owner ten dollars to buy, and for the want of them a slave which is worth a thousand dollars dies from cold and exposure; or for the want of proper food, may sicken and die in the same way. Thus, we see that men who grow rich fastest by the labor of their slaves, invariably feed and clothe them better than those whose slaves are of but little value. All who are in the habit of managing negro slaves, know that they do not regard work, and that they even delight in it when they are properly fed and clothed.

The owner should also look after his overseers or managers frequently, and see if they treat the negroes properly, and never suffer his slaves to be treated in any cruel or unusual ill manner. Some overseers, particularly green ones, who know but little about managing slaves, and there are a great many of this kind who offer their services for such business, think that they must always be whipping and beating the slave, and, not having any judgment in such matters, sometimes kill the slave, or disable him, so as to render him valueless. Such a course of conduct is the best evidence of the want of qualification in an overseer; and I would say to slaveholders, If you have such a one, discharge him immediately; he will do you more harm than good; for all good managers get on smoothly without much noise or whipping. There is a great deal in management, and the overseer who understands his duties best, can the more easily impart a knowledge of duty to others. If you find that your overseer is a treacherous scamp, that he has betrayed or deceived you willfully in any instance, discharge him—he will deceive and betray you again; trust him no further. But if, on the other hand, you find that he is faithful and true; that he has a correct knowledge of his business; that everything moves on well under his management; and that he treats your slaves properly, and is devoted to your interest, retain him if possible—he is one in a thousand; and give him just as high wages as you can possibly afford, rather than part with him; for, be assured, it will puzzle you to get another to fill his place; and occasionally, though rare, we find one of this kind.

The overseer will be certain in all cases to be more particular, and strive harder to please, when he sees his employer taking an interest in the farm, and looking into his management. The owner should occasionally inspect the negro-houses and their clothes and bedding, and see that they are well supplied, and everything kept neat; and in the winter season, particularly in very cold weather, have wood hauled in great abundance and placed near their houses, to enable them to keep good fires; they should also never suffer mothers to be separated from their children under ten years of age, but keep the mothers on the same farm where the children are, winter and summer; for the mothers will be certain to take better care of their children than any other person would, and in cold weather it is often necessary for mothers to rise in the night and cover up their children, in order to keep them from freezing; when they are willing to wait on their own children in this way, they would be unwilling to wait upon the children of others, and would let them lie and freeze rather than be troubled with them.

Sometimes it is the case that guardians or administrators, in the South, have negroes to hire out, which belong to the estate of the intestate or their wards, among whom there are women and children; in such cases it is far better to hire all of the children under twelve years old with their mothers, and if the woman has a husband to be hired, it is better to hire the husband with his wife and children all together in one lot, with an express condition that they are not to be separated or rehired without the written consent of the owner or guardian. Although in such cases they may hire for less money, they will certainly be better taken care of, and of more value at the end of the year, than they would be hired separate, and less liable to die when sick for the want of attention.

The owners of slaves should always act toward the slave in such a manner as to insure his respect and reverence. Therefore, he ought never to use any undue familiarity with his slave; for if he becomes too familiar with him, he will be certain to lose his respect. He should be kind and humane to his slave, and correct his faults in such a manner as not to be cruel. He should always be prompt with him, and be sure to perform all of his promises to him; pay him everything he promises with a degree of punctuality, so as to induce his slave to think it impossible for his owner to deceive him; and never show any vindictiveness whatever. Whenever you have to chastise him, do it in such a manner as to show him it is done to correct his faults and make him obey, as a parent would his child, and not from any feeling of vindictive vengeance; and in this way you will have the love and esteem of your slaves, make them fond of their home, and devoted to your interest.

If at any time you should own a vindictive slave—and it is sometimes the case—and you think yourself in danger from him, or any number of them, always be prepared for a controversy, but never let them know that you are afraid of them; but, on the contrary, always pretend as though you thought yourself perfectly safe, and they will not be half so apt to make an attack upon you.

Negro slaves, as I have observed before, when properly treated and properly governed, are as useful and necessary as any other class of human beings, and are the main root which extracts from the earth the principal sustenance which goes to the support of all of the balance of the human race; but, when badly governed, or left to themselves, of all others they are of the least value, and like all other savages the most dangerous. When let loose to a free exercise of their passions and feelings, their brutal barbarity knows no bounds, as has been illustrated on several occasions, where an attempt was made at insurrection in several parts of the United States, and other places. Nothing short of total extermination ever satisfies their savage desires; and awful have been the scenes where they have been successful in their insurrections.

Therefore, the owners of negro slaves cannot be too cautious in pursuing that course, in the government of their slaves, which will keep down insurrection, and the best promote the happiness of the slave, the welfare, the interest, and the safety of the slaveholder.

CHAPTER XVII.

Free Negroes, and their Influence and Danger among Slaves.

Negro slaves should, in all cases, be kept as far from any vile influence operating on their minds as possible. If possible, they should not be permitted to talk or even think of being free. It should always be made to appear to them that the black man and the mulatto were born to be slaves to the white people; and, therefore, they should never be permitted to see a free negro or mulatto. Such a thing ought not to exist in a slave country where there are negro slaves; if it does, it is always attended with the most serious consequences. The very presence of one free negro or free mulatto in the slaveholding part of the United States, will do more to breed insurrection among the slaves, and render them discontented with their condition, than one hundred abolition presses in the North, where there are no slaves. Although the free negro or mulatto may be a clever man, and not at all disposed to do wrong, the slaves will look on him and compare their own condition with that of the free negro, and desire to be free as well as he is—and thus his very presence will breed disaffection.

Yet we see, in some of our Southern slaveholding cities, free negroes and free mulattoes strutting about with impunity, smoking their cigars in the market-places, and wielding a gold-headed cane, with as much consequence as if they were the governors of the country; and all this is tolerated as a matter of little consequence, when a great noise and commotion is made about the abolitionists in Massachusetts and other non-slaveholding places, as being great bugbears and dangerous enemies to the slave and slaveholder. In this way, you pass by the substance and strike at the shadow. If you wish to be safe—if you wish your negroes to be satisfied with their condition—if you wish to put down every inducement to insurrection among the negroes—if you wish, with your families, your wives, your daughters, and your children, to be in safety by your own fireside, which it is your imperative duty to do, remove every free negro and free mulatto out of the bounds of the slaveholding region; send them to Liberia or some of the free States, and never suffer a free negro or free mulatto to enter the slaveholding region. If one is set free among you, send him immediately out of the country. If they settle among the abolitionists in the free States, they will soon get tired of them, and wish them back in the slave States, and soon shut their mouths about abolitionism. But by no means permit a free negro or mulatto to remain among you, neither permit any negro to hire his own time, and stroll through the country seeking employment, under severe penalties. This is the only way you can be secure, in the enjoyment of your negro property in the South; and, although in a few cases it may seem hard to compel the free negroes to emigrate and leave their old friends and acquaintances, yet it is far better for them to do so, and make some sacrifices, than that a whole community should suffer, and, in consequence of their presence, be in continual danger of having the country deluged in blood from an insurrection occasioned by the influence of their remaining.

CHAPTER XVIII.

The Conclusion, with Seven Maxims as Advice to Young Men.

In conclusion, I feel that I have been wonderfully protected, in the many different scenes in life through which I have had to pass, by the Omnipotent hand of God, in whom I trust for present comfort and future happiness. At a very early age I had serious and religious impressions, and frequently, when I was but a child, retired in secret to implore the aid and forgiveness of Him who rules the universe—the great God, from whom all blessings flow; through whose mercy and goodness, by the mediation of Jesus Christ, my Saviour, I hope to inherit eternal life, to whom be all glory and honor and power forever;—for I feel that God has heard my prayers, and answered them on many and various occasions, and that I am the special object of his care and protection. Without his assistance, I should be nothing; and with his help, I am enabled to stand.

Now, I have a few words to say to young men, in conclusion, which, if they will take heed to, will prove a jewel and a fortune:—

1st. Shun intoxicating liquor as you would a poisonous viper; for thousands have fallen victims to its use; neither touch, taste, or handle the unclean thing.

2d. Shun the card-table as you would a rattlesnake: it allures, charms, and then destroys its victim. Never risk at play that which will make your family comfortable.

3d. Endeavor to keep out of bad company; for men are judged by the company they keep.

4th. Never put off until to-morrow any of your business that you can attend to to-day; for men often lose much by neglecting their business; for to-morrow has business enough for itself, without engrossing the business of to-day.

5th. Never forsake an old, tried, and faithful friend for a new one.

6th. Don't forget to read the Bible as much as you can, because in it we read what is necessary to make us happy here and hereafter. It is the best book in the world, and is the inestimable gift of God to man.

7th. And above all, worship God and keep his commandments: this is not only our duty, but a very high privilege.

FINIS.

www.ingramcontent.com/pod-product-compliance
Lightning Source LLC
Chambersburg PA
CBHW020831230426
43666CB00007B/1179